THE PREDICTION OF CRIMINAL BEHAVIOUR: STATISTICAL APPROACHES

As Western societies struggle with a deepening crisis of violence and the apparent failure of our penal systems to reduce crimes, increasing attention is paid to the identification of potentially violent behaviour before it erupts.

Thomas Gabor advances our understanding of the techniques for predicting criminal behaviour and the ethical and practical issues surrounding them. He discusses the uses of prediction in bail, sentencing, and parole decisions, as well as in the allocation of treatments to offenders. He offers a review of current research on the statistical methods, and presents a typology of predictive approaches. This typology serves as the framework for a discussion of the various predictive factors, including sex, race and ethnicity, age, personality and intelligence, socio-economic status, criminal history, institutional adjustment, drug and alcohol use, the family, peer influences, and situational factors. Each of these is assessed in terms of both its value in predicting criminality and its propriety from an ethical point of view.

Gabor also deals with the way in which the variables in prediction are statistically combined. He discusses the issues of variable measurement and sampling in considerable detail, and considers some of the statistical methods most commonly used to predict criminality, including the Burgess Method, predictive attributive analysis, multiple regression, multidiscriminant analysis, and log-linear techniques. He concludes with an evaluation of the potential value of statistical predictions in the development of theories and criminal justice policies and practices, based on statistical and ethical considerations.

The result is a comprehensive overview of an increasingly important area of statistical application.

THOMAS GABOR is a professor in the Department of Criminology, University of Ottawa.

THOMAS GABOR

The Prediction of Criminal Behaviour: Statistical Approaches

UNIVERSITY OF TORONTO PRESS
Toronto Buffalo London

© University of Toronto Press 1986
Toronto Buffalo London
Printed in Canada

ISBN 0-8020-5691-1

Printed on acid-free paper

Canadian Cataloguing in Publication Data
Gabor, Thomas.
The predictability of criminal behaviour

Bibliography: p.
Includes index.
ISBN 0-8020-5691-1

1. Criminal behaviour, Prediction of – Statistical
methods. I. Title.

HV6018.G33 1986   364.4 '1 '028   C86-093631-7

This book has been published with the help of a grant from the Social Sciences
Federation of Canada, using funds provided by the Social Sciences and
Humanities Research Council of Canada.

Contents

To Sy Dinitz and Ed Sagarin,
with profound gratitude and respect

Acknowledgments

I am indebted to many persons and agencies in the completion of this book. To attempt to enumerate them all would only make oversights more conspicuous. I shall therefore endeavour only to mention those most instrumental in bringing this work to fruition.

First and foremost, I am deeply grateful for all the efforts of Dr Simon Dinitz of Ohio State University. It was he who originally stimulated my interest in prediction when he invited me to join the Dangerous Offender Project at the Academy for Contemporary Problems in 1979. Since then, he has tirelessly and unselfishly supported this project all the way through to its publication. His scholarly advice, ability to motivate, and compassion were absolutely indispensable to me.

Dr Ed Sagarin, now a Visiting Distinguished Professor at the University of Delaware, has been advising me in my work on prediction and dangerousness for almost as long. It was my very good fortune that he arrived on the Ohio State campus in the spring of 1981 just as I was embarking upon this work. I was immediately impressed by the interest he took in it and have since continually been encouraged by the manner in which he has monitored its progress. I learned a great deal from his meticulous reviews of the various drafts that I submitted to him. In fact, both Drs Dinitz and Sagarin worked with me for so long on this project and read so many drafts that they might have easily predicted that it would never come to publication. Instead, their enthusiasm and faith in me were an inspiration, creating a self-fulfilling prophecy.

I am also grateful for the advice and support of my current colleagues, as well as for the financial assistance provided me by the Department of Criminology at the University of Ottawa. Other sources of funding came from three doctoral fellowships at the inception of the project and, more recently, from a publication grant by the Social Sciences Federation of Canada. The comments made on the manuscript by the various anonymous reviewers were invaluable. The copy-editing skills of Mr John Parry of the University of Toronto Press were very beneficial. I am also deeply appreciative of the unselfish and meticulous editorial assistance of my close friend, Ms Tonia Barker.

Finally, I would like to thank my parents for their unflagging support throughout the course of this project. They have provided me with the motivation and vitality for this and future works.

THE PREDICTION OF CRIMINAL BEHAVIOUR

Introduction

Policy-makers today are torn between the dual objectives of criminal justice systems. On the one hand, there is the utilitarian goal of crime prevention which has become a high priority because of the nearly universal increases in serious traditional or 'street' crime beginning in the 1960s (Radzinowicz and King 1977). Also, findings from criminological research have indicated that a small proportion of criminals are responsible for a disproportionately large amount of crime (Wolfgang, Figlio, and Sellin 1972), inspiring a focus on the factors that might identify these hard-core offenders as early in their illicit careers as possible. On the other hand, the abuses and limitations of such practices as coercive treatment and the indeterminate sentence (American Friends Service Committee 1972; Mitford 1974) have led to a strong resurgence of the retributive or justice-oriented approach to dealing with crime (Fogel 1979; Frankel 1972; Singer 1979; von Hirsch 1976). This approach emphasizes the moral aspects of criminal justice interventions, and its major thrust is the introduction of equity in the sentencing process.

These concurrent and seemingly incompatible trends have pointed to the need for a compromise between merely denouncing offenders and demanding expiation for acts that are a fait accompli and an unfettered pragmatism aiming to neutralize offenders (especially the dangerous) at any cost. One compromise might take the form of developing more standardized criteria for decision-makers, with these criteria accommodating both retributive and utilitarian goals. In this way not only might the prediction and prevention of criminal behaviour be enhanced, but decisions would also be based on more equitable criteria: similar standards could be applied across cases. Such criteria could also include retributive considerations (e.g., whether a person has a prior criminal record). Where retribution is irrelevant or less paramount, as in pre-trial release and parole decisions, the aim could be to develop guidelines to assist decision-makers responsible for predicting offenders' behaviour. Such guidelines might maximize the likelihood of making an appropriate decision and enhance the credibility of the criminal justice system. Predictive decisions based on specified criteria, which are developed and validated through empirical methods and rely primarily on criminal justice data, are of the actuarial or statistical type. The other major mode of prediction, while not entirely distinct from the statistical type, is the clinical. It is with statistical prediction that most of our concern rests. The credibility of clinical predictions of criminal behaviour has declined considerably in recent years (Monahan 1981).

Predictions in the context of criminal justice serve three basic purposes. First, they can help assess the potential danger an individual poses to society. Second, they can ascertain the level of custody or surveillance required in the management of an offender in the care of a correctional institution or agency. Third, they assess the therapeutic needs of an offender. The major concern here centres around the first-mentioned function. Prediction in the form of forecasting trends in crime will not be considered.

Crime prevention can be enhanced by predictions made at various points in the criminal justice system and even beyond it. Predictions can help nip crime in the bud if they aid in the early identification of those persons and groups most prone to criminal behaviour. Ethical dilemmas may abound in these efforts, as they may result in the adoption of such extreme measures as the incapacitation or quarantine of some persons prior to their commission of any criminal act. The argument has been made that preventive confinement has always existed in Anglo-American legal systems through such mechanisms as pre-trial detention, vagrancy laws, status offences, and laws governing attempted criminal acts (Dershowitz 1974; Packer 1968). Nevertheless, the routine application of preventive detention would undoubtedly be regarded by many with a great deal of trepidation.

Guidelines for predictions have been established to aid courts in bail decisions and sentencing, parole boards in release decisions, and correctional personnel in the classification of offenders.

At the level of decisions regarding the granting of bail, the key issue is whether an accused will appear in court or abscond. The Vera Institute of Justice in New York has devised perhaps the best-known criteria for predicting offender behaviour in this regard (Ares, Rankin, and Sturz 1963). Among the leading factors predicting court appearance have been the residential stability of offenders, their community ties, their employment record, and their criminal history.

Guidelines for sentencing have been established in many jurisdictions. In

Ohio, for example, juvenile court judges have followed a sentencing model that considers both the nature of the current offence and offender characteristics in their decision about whether to place a youth in an institution (Juvenile Court Judges of Ohio 1979). The predictive component of the placement decision is captured by the offender score provided for each juvenile. This score is based primarily on variables relating to the prior misconduct of a youth. The mean seriousness of previous offences is calculated on the basis of a severity rating scale; total and serious prior offences are tallied, as are previous institutional commitments, and the presence of a drug or alcohol problem is considered. If an offender scores high on the variables relating to previous conduct and susceptibility to substance abuse, he or she would be considered a high risk to release into the community.

Proposals to include predictions explicitly in sentencing reached their apex when serious consideration was given to the policy of selective incapacitation. Proponents of this policy assert that criminal sentences should be individualized, with the overriding aim being the neutralization of the offender. They claim that prisons do not rehabilitate or even deter potential offenders from committing crimes. Radical proponents of this policy regard prisons as little more than warehouses from which inmates emerge in roughly the same shape they entered. They rely on a substantial body of empirical evidence to support their claim that prison does not have demonstrated adverse effects on criminal behaviour after an offender's release from an institution. Thus they suggest that all we can hope for is to make the criminal justice system more efficient through the optimal use of correctional resources. This situation can be achieved, they say, by being more selective in our imposition of prison sentences.

Concretely, such a policy, in its more doctrinaire form, would involve sentencing offenders according to the risk they pose to society rather than according to the gravity of their most recent offences, as entailed by the traditional justice model. Predictive models, such as that devised by Greenwood and Abrahamse (1982), would be developed to classify offenders, the ultimate goal being to incapacitate or neutralize the most active and dangerous offenders.

Modified incapacitation policies have been implemented in the United States in the form of career offender programs (Chelimsky and Dahmann 1981) and mandatory sentences for offences such as armed robbery. Career offender programs target habitual criminals through additional prosecutorial resources, and mandatory sentences are designed to diminish dramatically the incidence of specific serious crimes. Career offender programs use predictive criteria to identify candidates for whom special processing is required.

In addition, many countries have 'dangerous offender,' 'sexual psychopath,' and related legislation that calls for indeterminate sentences for those falling within the ambit of these laws (Petrunik 1980). These statutes have often been intended to cover extremely violent and/or abnormal offenders for whom fixed penalties, with the possibility of release into the community, might be inappropriate. On many occasions and in a variety of countries, the original intent of these statutes has been undermined, as petty property offenders and non-violent sex offenders have been the targets of draconian sentences (Bottoms 1977; Greenland 1984).

One phase in the criminal justice process in which prediction is vital is that regarding the decision to grant or deny parole. The United States Parole Commission, for example, has used a matrix or grid of guidelines that considers both the nature of an inmate's most recent offence and an offender risk dimension (salient factor score) (Gottfredson, Wilkins, and Hoffman 1978). The more serious the offence, the longer the offender will serve, his or her characteristics remaining constant. Similarly, the lower the salient factor score, the longer he will serve, the nature of the offence remaining constant. This offender score is calculated on the basis of such variables as a person's number of prior convictions and incarcerations, age at first commitment to an institution, presence or absence of substance abuse, education, employment history, and release plan.

Guidelines have also been developed to aid probation and parole agencies, as well as correctional institutions, in determining the appropriate levels of supervision or security for offenders, based on their expected conduct in the community or in custody. In Wisconsin, probationers and parolees have been assessed for risk on the basis of such factors as residential stability, recent employment record, use of alcohol or drugs, attitude, age at first conviction, number of prior serious offences, and presence or absence of probation or parole revocations (Baird, Heinz, and Bemus 1978). At six-month intervals, offenders on probation or parole are reassessed to determine whether their status has changed. The reassessment schedule shifts in emphasis from the criminal history items stressed in the risk assessment at intake to the offender's response to the legally imposed conditions of probation or parole, his use of community resources, and his interpersonal relationships. Also, the updated status of his employment record, residential stability, and drug or alcohol problems is gauged.

Innumerable classification schemes have been devised for the placement of offenders in the most appropriate institutional situation, bearing in mind the dual objectives of custody and rehabilitation (American Correctional Association 1975). This placement is most often based on such factors as the potential security problem posed by the inmate, medical and psychiatric needs, age, criminal sophistication, and safety, as well as the safety of other inmates (Bartollas and Miller 1978). The use of such criteria is based on the assumption that more arbitrary placements will produce an increase in institutional disorder and the disruption of correctional programs.

Aside from these formal predictions at various points in the criminal justice system, the identification of groups and persons most susceptible to criminality may be desired to enhance efforts at secondary crime prevention (Brantingham and Faust 1976). These may range from social-psychological interventions to the quarantine of those highly prone to dangerous behaviour. The latter has been referred to as 'universal preventive detention,' because any person, irrespective of his actual conduct, may be eligible for incapacitative measures designed to protect society (von Hirsch 1976). The controversy accompanying such a policy would be profound, as it would violate both the presumption-of-innocence principle, as well as the presumption that a person is harmless until proven otherwise (Floud and Young 1981).

Notwithstanding these objections, the preventive confinement of persons considered to be dangerous has, even in Western countries, always been practised in some form (Dershowitz 1974). Status offences and vagrancy laws are examples of statutes that either explicitly or in practice have upheld society's right to intervene without the actual commission of a criminal act (Packer 1968). Pre-trial detention is also an example of a penal intervention in the absence of demonstrated culpability. Ordinarily, this form of detention is intended not as a quarantine measure but as a means to ensure the appearance of an accused for trial when this is not expected to occur (Shattuck and Landau 1981).

Attempts to identify a disposition towards criminality were initially stimulated by Sheldon and Eleanor Glueck. In *Unraveling Juvenile Delinquency*, they developed predictors of delinquent behaviour that could be employed on the entrance of children into elementary school (Glueck and Glueck 1950). Specifically, they focused on family dynamics – parental discipline, supervision, affection, and family cohesiveness. Although their methods were heavily criticized, a substantial number of attempts have been made to validate their social prediction table (Weis 1974).

The efforts of the Gluecks and other pioneers in criminological prediction have been followed by countless other attempts to isolate the individual traits or environmental factors that drive people towards, and hence predict their involvement in, crime. These studies underline another important function of prediction: to enhance the development of criminological theory. Prediction studies have included a multitude of variables, have combined them with varying degrees of sophistication, and have achieved different levels of success. On the whole, however, the prediction enterprise has proved to be of limited success. An exploration of the reasons for the failures is one of the principal objectives of this work. For a detailed treatment of the evolution of prediction in criminology and a discussion of the studies, the reader is referred to the work of Mannheim and Wilkins (1965) and Frances H. Simon (1971).

Despite ethical concerns and limited success, predictive devices become more palatable perhaps when one considers that most human behaviour already includes some anticipative or predictive element. Prediction is a routine human preoccupation, inherent in all social behaviour. It is frequently a subtle process intertwined with many other considerations. Thus the decision to turn on a light switch is based on the expectation that the action will result in the illumination of a room. However, it is based not merely on that expectation, but on the relative strength of the motive(s) to enter the room as opposed to undertaking some alternative action(s). Where prediction is less reliable, it is more difficult to discern its relative importance in the ultimate decision to act in a certain manner. This is particularly true in criminal justice, where competing rationales for decisions exist on both the formal and informal levels. Observers of its processes indicate, however, that a predictive element is almost always involved (Hogarth 1971).

Formal efforts in prediction are hampered by the often capricious responses of criminal justice systems and the public towards illicit behaviour. Since the independent and dependent variables in criminological prediction are often measured on the basis of official records, the more these are randomly or systematically distorted, the less they reflect the actual behaviour of offenders. The more extensive these biases, the greater the likelihood that the predictive power of the independent variables will be minimal. If predictive power is maintained despite such distortion, this may be because social reactions themselves are predictable and it is these that are being registered. Alternatively, these distortions may be so randomly distributed that the official data actually reflect the characteristics and behaviour of the relevant offender population.

Suppose we were predicting parole outcome for a group of inmates on the basis of their previous criminal conduct. In order to determine the factors most likely to affect parole success, we first develop a predictive model based on the criminal records of, say, 1,000 former parolees. We then perform a multiple correlation analysis, using this sample of 1,000, to ascertain which factors (in combination) are most closely associated with and, hence, predictive of parole success. Let us say that we find the most potent predictive factors to be number of prior offences, absence of drug or alcohol-related crimes, age at first conviction, and institutional behaviour.

All these measures, including that of parole success, are inadequate in some ways. People classified as being successful on parole may actually have committed violations but may, simply, not have been detected. Conversely, those classified as failures may merely have committed very technical violations (e.g., been seen with persons they were ordered not to associate with) detected by an overzealous parole officer. If these two forms of misclassification occur in an approximately equal number of cases, then the relative proportion of parole successes and failures in the sample will not be altered. This might be called random error because the misclassifications, in a sense, cancel out. If these errors are numerous, however, they will likely reduce the magnitude of the correlations with the predictor variables and, hence, understate their predictive value. More systematic forms of error occur when, as a result of policy, one of these types of error is more likely to occur than the other. The recorded distribution of parole successes and failures, in that case, no longer reflects the true distribution.

These same issues pertain to the independent (predictor) variables mentioned. We might err in relation to a person's drug or alcohol use and institutional conduct. The age at which an offender was first arrested or convicted may or may not reflect the age at which he or she actually embarked on a criminal career. If each offender is convicted exactly three years following the actual onset of his career, then using the age at first conviction as a measure will not seriously alter the predictive power of the age variable, as the rank-order of the sample on this variable will not change. However, if our measurement error is less systematic, and some offenders are apprehended on their first offence, while others are apprehended only four or five years later, their status on the variable is as dependent on the fortuitous circumstances of getting caught as on actual offender behaviour.

The variable 'number of prior convictions' is similar. When we use criminal records to predict recidivism or parole outcome, we know that the offences registered in an offender's file tend to constitute a low estimate of the actual level of his criminal activity. We do not know, however, how low an estimate it is. An intelligent or opportunistic offender, operating in a sprawling urban environment in which police clearance rates are low, may commit hundreds of offences before being caught. However, a narcotics addict who is not as selective in choosing crime targets and who may even be under the influence of drugs during the commission of crimes may be apprehended at a far higher rate. If there are such differences in apprehension rates among offenders, offender files may contain biased information on the extent of a criminal career. Further, the scope of this bias would be unknown.

It is in this sense that predictions based on police, court, and other official records are sensitive to the consistency and efficiency of criminal justice system policies. A criminal act is recorded only if it is detected, interpreted as criminal, and followed by action on the part of law enforcement officials.

Some of the factors contributing to the arbitrariness of the system's responses to anti-social behaviour are outside its control. The crime-reporting practices of the public and the definitions conferred on social behaviour in varying situational and normative contexts are hardly amenable to control. Similarly, human errors in arresting and convicting the innocent, as well as failures in apprehending or convicting the culpable, will inevitably persist. The arbitrary and whimsical behaviour of criminal justice personnel is another matter (Frankel 1972). The behaviour of these decision-makers has been found, at times, to be as unpredictable as that of offenders.

In an examination of sentences received by 1,138 violent juvenile offenders in Columbus, Ohio, Hamparian and her colleagues (1978, 111) concluded: 'All the "hard" quantifiable type variables, taken singly or in combination, with or without interaction effects, explain little of the variation in disposition. If nothing more, this study affirms that the soft, subjective variables – quality of family attachment, interest, and cohesion – were "better" predictors of individual arrest outcome than the traditional categories that are included in most predictive tables.' Bottomley (1973), in England, has arrived at a similar conclusion. In a study of parole decisions relating to 207 prison inmates, factors such as the prisoner's personality and attitudes had greater weight than those relating to criminal history, family situation, and employment prospects. Clearly, an emphasis on such subjective factors as the demeanour of the offender will perpetuate disparities in dispositions for offenders with objectively similar characteristics.

In Canada, Hogarth (1971), through interviews with 71 magistrates in Ontario, concerning 1,103 criminal cases, found weak correlations between magistrates' perceptions of the facts of a case and the length of the sentences they imposed. In Israel, Shoham (1966) examined the sentencing practices of nine judges in three district courts and concluded that the great variation between judges, in sentences imposed, could be attributed only to attitudinal and dispositional differences on their part. Regional differences in sentencing (Jaffary 1963), and ethnic, racial, and sex discrimination (Hagan 1974; Kratcoski 1974; Meade 1973; Piliavin and Briar 1964), also point to a capricious system. The elimination of these disparate practices is a necessary first step in enhancing predictive efforts.

Statistical prediction is of dubious value if the data on which it is based fail to reflect actual patterns of offender behaviour. Of course, other sources of data can be tapped to understand offender behaviour for the ultimate purpose of making predictions. Interviews with offenders and victims (self-report and victim surveys, respectively), as well as observational studies, are more costly procedures for learning about offender behaviour, and they are objected to on grounds other than the criticisms generally levelled at official criminal statistics. Some of the studies to be discussed have employed these other means of discerning offender behaviour patterns. Their common advantage over official data sources is that they circumvent the criminal justice system and, consequently, are not sensitive to the inaccuracies or prejudices of criminal justice personnel and to spasmodic shifts in policy.

1

Dangers, limitations, and ethical dilemmas in prediction

In developing a predictive instrument (e.g. parole decision tables) for decision-makers in the criminal justice system, the researcher should be aware of the variety of uses to which the scheme may be applied, the criteria according to which its efficacy will be appraised, and its potential impact on all parties affected by its application. Equally fundamental, however, are considerations relating to the 'marketing' of the instrument itself; unfortunately, meticulous method and predictive reliability are insufficient.

In attempting to sell a predictive system to policy-makers, the researcher may be tempted to incorporate social utility, as opposed to sheer accuracy, as a principal component of the system (Ascher 1978). Thus, if he or she finds that race is a good predictor of recidivism and partly attributes this to the prejudicial treatment of minorities at all stages of the criminal justice system, the researcher may overadjust for this factor, believing that erring on the liberal side might at least rectify, to some degree, inequities in the system. Thus, if members of a particular minority group were twice as likely to be arrested and have their offences recorded as were members of other groups engaging in the same level of illegal activity, those devising parole guidelines, for example, might justifiably compensate for such discrimination by establishing different institutional release criteria for the minority group. Thus, four prior arrests in the file of a person facing such discrimination might be considered equivalent to two arrests in the files of other inmates. The problem is that changing decision criteria does not translate to changes in enforcement practices in the real world. Even if members of this group were no more likely to commit additional crimes on release, their subsequent offences would more likely be registered than those of others. If persons with an adjusted (diminished) criminal record are often found to recidivate or violate parole, the credibility of the predictive guidelines would be set back vis-à-vis the policy establishment. At the same time, the public's faith in the criminal justice system would not be enhanced.

A different danger is posed by the possibility that the policy-maker, enthusiastic about a predictive system, adopts it as his or her own and uses it to promote his own occupational position and ideological perspective. A scheme can thereby evolve from a project aiming to improve the accuracy of prediction to an object of vested interests (Ascher 1978).

The researcher must also anticipate the different uses to which a predictive system may be applied, as well as the specific needs and capabilities of the practitioner. Such an instrument may serve as a mere guideline to decisions, it may structure discretion, or its use may itself be discretionary. However, policy may require a mechanical adherence to the scheme, the 'decision-maker' serving the role of a mere accountant. If people are made to feel dehumanized, resistance undermining the entire system can be anticipated. If 'sentencing by computers' were ever introduced, for example, a compensating increase in judicial control over criminal procedure might occur.

Also relevant to the proper application of formal predictive devices/ tables are simplicity and parsimony (Mannheim and Wilkins 1955). A device requiring a multitude of information relating to the offender presupposes the establishment of a data-gathering apparatus to obtain such information. In the absence of such resources, the user may merely circumvent tedious segments of the scheme, while placing disproportionate weight on items for which abundant information is available.

Errors in prediction are inevitable, and their costs cannot be measured in absolute terms. One can develop prediction cutting points (i.e. prediction decision criteria) that minimize the total number of false positive and negative errors (Dunn 1980). A false positive is the erroneous belief that one has a given attribute or propensity (e.g. dangerousness), and a false negative error is the mistaken belief that one does not. False positives have been called errors of inefficiency, as they result in the delivery of services (including custody) to those not requiring them. False negatives are errors of ineffectiveness, as needs for services are not met (Bryan D. Jones 1980).

The ramifications of committing either type of error depend on the type of criminal behaviour involved. The cost of a false negative, clearly, is substantially higher in the case of a violent offender than in that of a habitual shoplifter. The cost of a false positive, at first glance, would appear to be higher with respect to the shoplifter, because the risk, in the event he or she does recidivate, is rather low. Thus, erroneously predicting recidivism for a petty property offender results in needless expenditures, because the risk of withholding these expenditures is low. However, the cost of needlessly providing services for a convicted violent offender are offset by the potential catastrophic consequences of erroneously releasing him or her from custody. In absolute terms, however, the cost of falsely detaining such an individual exceeds that for the petty offender, as tighter security measures are required for his or her detention (Nagel and Neef 1979). The cost of false positives may, paradoxically, undermine public security if the costs incurred by a correctional system consume resources (e.g. prison space) to the point where the thresholds of violence at which false positive errors are tolerated are raised to alleviate the burden on the system. Thus, policies that are excessively prudent and insufficiently selective in the use of prison may produce such levels of overcrowding that dangerous offenders must be released prematurely or judges need to be more reluctant in resorting to incarceration.

The respective likelihood of committing false positive and false negative errors depends largely on the actual prevalence or base rate of the targeted behaviour. An increasing base rate, with the sensitivity of the predictive device held constant, will reduce the number of false positives and increase the likelihood of false negatives. A decreasing base rate will have the opposite effect. Generally speaking, base rates for violent behaviour, even in the United States, have been too low to permit accurate predictions of violent recidivism (Meehl and Rosen 1955; Monahan 1981). The closer the base rate in a population approximates 50 per cent, the greater the relevance of predictive schemes. Conversely, as the base rate of the targeted behaviour approaches either zero or 100 per cent, prediction in any particular case that the outcome will resemble that of the modal group in that population will be more reliable than a prediction based on the most sophisticated device. Thus, if only 5 per cent of persons in a particular population subgroup commit violent offences, the best prediction for anyone within that group is that he or she will not commit a violent offence. If, however, 95 per cent are violent, the best prediction is that of a violent outcome.

The generally low base rates of violence combined with the current interest in identifying dangerous offenders has resulted in a preoccupation, on the part of civil libertarians, with false positive errors. To be sure, there are examples of gross errors reported in the literature (Steadman and Keveles 1972; Wenk, Robinson, and Smith 1972). Also, we should not ignore the argument that cases of false positives have been swept under the rug because of the vested interests served by institutionalization and the political impotence of inmates (Monahan 1975). The notoriety of cases (particularly the sensational) involving the violent recidivism of purportedly rehabilitated individuals unquestionably overshadows the silent anguish of those unjustifiably subjected to detention.

Nevertheless, the number of false positives may be substantially overestimated in current studies. Most of these studies are based on circumstances in which clinical recommendations to confine suspected dangerous offenders were disregarded or where radical policy shifts occurred, resulting in a wholesale release of those destined for long-term confinement (Steadman and Keveles 1972; Kozol, Boucher, and Garofalo 1972). Some of those believed not to have recidivated after being identified as dangerous may actually have committed offences and avoided detention. In some studies, the follow-up period may have been insufficient to ensure that recidivism did not occur. Also, as Quinsey (1980) notes, the base rate of violence for prisoners may not be accurately gauged in any given year because those deemed too dangerous to be released at one point will be reconsidered on subsequent occasions and have an increasingly greater chance of being released. If this assumption is correct and one computes the base rate on the basis of cohorts, then the base rate increases in each successive year in the life of a cohort.

For those not released by fortuitous circumstances, these possibilities provide little consolation. The criminal justice system lacks feedback concerning decisions to confine. One can only speculate on the correctness of decisions concerning release. Such ambiguities easily lend themselves to rationalizations regarding the merits of institutionalization, particularly when the only concrete feedback to which criminal justice personnel are exposed involves cases of insufficient prudence (Monahan 1975).

Aside from the tautological nature of many such decisions, the predictive enterprise may foster self-fulfilling consequences as well (Ascher 1978). That is, predictions may produce actions that validate them. Thus, if the variable of race is believed to be a good predictor of recidivism and policies are based on this belief, the differential treatment subsequently accorded the relevant racial groups may themselves be responsible for the varying outcomes. This possible adverse consequence of prediction has led various writers (e.g. Frances H. Simon 1971) to caution us about the cavalier use of predictive instruments, particularly for vulnerable groups or people in their formative years. Predicting that a teenager will become a dangerous criminal may lead to his or her playing the role, especially if the reactions of others reinforce that role.

Predictions may also be self-defeating if measures are adopted to rectify problematic relationships (e.g. race and recidivism) identified by the projections. Paradoxically, a prediction may be invalidated by the resolution of a problem. Predictions may consequently be accurate at the time they are formulated and would remain so if the problem identified were ignored. However, reactions to troublesome predictions may occur and transform the original context. Thus, a finding that race was strongly associated with and, hence, predictive of a certain type of crime might result in the establishment of affirmative action programs. Such programs might ultimately correct the problem and thereby reduce our ability to predict the commission of that crime by our mere knowledge of an individual's race.

The designation of an act as criminal may change over time and vary from one context to another. This may be due to changing social values and/or changing law enforcement policies. Predictions are sensitive to such changes. An ex-inmate predicted to succeed on parole may be considered a failure merely because a sudden clamp-down occurs in relation to technical violations, rather than as a result of an unanticipated behaviour on his part.

Should predictions also attempt to incorporate anticipated societal reactions and policy changes? If they do so, they will invariably be confounding, integrating predictions of the targeted behaviour with different reaction scenarios. Conditional probability statements can accommodate the various scenarios (Ascher 1978).

Another limitation is the general exclusion of environmental factors from predictive efforts (Monahan 1981). Using the most comprehensive data on offender characteristics, one can achieve only limited success in explaining behaviour because of the dynamic, interpersonal nature of many criminal acts. Even if one presumed that an individual was 'predestined' to commit an offence, the time and location at which it is committed, its gravity, and the frequency of its repetition will be affected by such factors as situational stresses, availability of opportunities, weapons, and targets, and victim behaviour that arise between antecedent conditions and the commission of the offence.

Future behaviour does not constitute a mere projection of past events (Ascher 1978). Rather, new conditions and unanticipated events arise which, if not taken into account, will place an impenetrable ceiling on predictive accuracy. The task, thus, becomes one of monitoring events as they progress and considering newly obtained information (Ohlin 1951). Predictions cease to be useful, however, if they merely integrate current and past information, while lacking the capability to project at least fundamental relations into the future. The optimal solution, therefore, is to develop models that can be applied for a duration of time sufficient to justify the expenditure of resources involved in their development but that do not presuppose the continuation of trends and relations for an unrealistic period. It has been suggested that clinicians should be judged by their ability to predict imminent dangerousness following assessment, because they cannot reasonably be expected to anticipate the environment and situations to which a patient will be exposed at more remote points in the future (Werner, Rose and Yesavage 1983). For policy planning in criminology, some consensus exists on a maximum of three-year forecasts (Hasenpusch 1978).

Another impediment to predictions is the frequent ambiguity (particularly in the clinical realm) of predictor and criterion variables. The former are the variables used to make the prediction and the latter those being predicted. The use of subjective factors as predictors, or the use of unreliable indicators in which the standard measurement error is large, results either in the concealment of some indicators actually used or in the use of unintended indicators. The use of criterion variables such as 'dangerousness' adds to the ambiguity of predictions. Dangerousness, as has been pointed out, can refer to a variety of behaviours and attributes, as well as the interaction of these with environmental conditions (Monahan 1981). Whenever dangerousness is being predicted or assessed, the specific behavioural referents of the term need to be delineated. A broad conception of clinicians of the properties of dangerousness invites circular thinking about the prognosis of an offender. As Monahan (1981) asserts, the clinician assessing a habitual offender for mental disturbance may believe that all such offenders are disturbed. The outcome of such an assessment is quite predictable.

The use of predictions for both civil and criminal court decisions has been contested on practical as well as ethical grounds (Monahan 1981). The practical objection centres around the limitations of past predictive efforts. Civil libertarians also claim that the individual should be punished for previous behaviour rather than for that which is anticipated.

Monahan (1984, 12) counters the civil libertarians by saying that while 'the prediction of recidivism is a Herculean task, the assessment of culpability is a divine one.' Thus those who point to the failures of prediction in commitments to psychiatric institutions or criminal justice decisions often ignore the subjectivity involved in the assessment of moral culpability subsumed within a legalistic, retributive sentencing model. Such a justice-oriented model assumes that all people are free to act as they choose, unless demonstrated otherwise; that they have equal opportunity to engage in lawful activity; and, hence, that they are equally blameworthy for illicit activity. Socio-economic deprivations and discrimination are not considered as mitigating factors in moral culpability. Also, the retributivists, while interested in meting out justice to offenders for their past crimes, do not consider the rights of future victims of these same offenders. Monahan does not quarrel with the principle of commensurate deserts, whereby sentences are proportional to the gravity of the offence committed. However, he believes that a justice-oriented sentencing scheme should be flexible enough to accommodate predictions about an offender's future behaviour (Monahan 1982).

The prediction of dangerousness on the part of mental health professionals is another difficult area. Professionals might be faced with a role-conflict situation, as they are expected to perform simultaneously therapeutic and social control functions. From the point of view of the 'client,' social control usually becomes paramount. The ambiguous nature of clinical assessments also tends to bring social control to the fore. The assessed individual may be subjected to a 'double-bind' situation whereby behaviour or mannerisms will be construed as symptomatic of some form of aberration. The refusal to accept the role of 'mentally ill' may be regarded as indicative of the person's failure to, as yet, come to terms with and work through his problems. However, the adoption of such a role and its concomitants may assure a poor prognosis (Goffman 1961).

It would appear that decisions regarding the loss of liberty (perhaps for indefinite periods), with all their ramifications in terms of social stigma, should be based on clear criteria, and decision-makers should be held accountable. The issue of accountability distinguishes statistical from other forms of prediction: decision-makers are not given carte blanche to select and define predictor and outcome variables as they see fit, nor do theoretical leanings and personal biases intrude as readily. The characteristics of statistical and other approaches to prediction, as well as their differences, are explored in the next chapter.

2

The dimensions of prediction

Predictions range from the highly systematic to those devoid of any basis in logic or fact (see figure). Systematic prediction involves an attempt to identify empirically the best predictive factors, to define these as well as the criterion (that which is being predicted) operationally, to evaluate and update the scheme periodically, and to minimize measurement error through ensuring that independent users (observers) will draw the same conclusions in the assessment of any given case. This is the issue of inter-rater reliability.

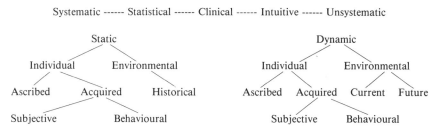

The dimensions of prediction

At the other end of the continuum are predictions strongly imbued with personal prejudices and perceptual distortions, lacking specificity as to outcome criteria and independent verification of their accuracy. In fact, a person may often be unaware of the fact that he or she is making a prediction or of its role in a decision he or she takes. In preparing a pre-sentence report, a probation officer, fearing that release of an offender would endanger the community, might selectively seek and attend to evidence that justifies the recommendation of a custodial sentence. He may be entirely unaware of the role that his fears have played in colouring his perception of facts relating to the case.

The two fundamental approaches to prediction are the statistical and the clinical. Although these approaches are not mutually exclusive (Monahan 1981), it is useful to consider them separately. Statistical prediction would typically fall more closely towards the 'systematic' end of our continuum than would clinical prediction, because it is based on more objectively discernible information and provides statistical statements regarding the predictive criterion that can be more readily subjected to validation. Clinical predictions include more subjective factors in assessment (Halleck 1967) and provide more general and, at times, ambiguous prognoses. They can, however, be considered more systematic than that of the probation officer just mentioned. This is because clinical prediction rests on theoretical models of human behaviour, conforms to some extent, at least, to established assessment and classificatory procedures, and is generally undertaken by people with clinical training presumed to be sensitive to factors potentially biasing their assessment. The extent to which a prediction is systematic should not be confused with its accuracy or precision.

Next, predictions can be distinguished by the type of indicators used for both the predictor and criterion variables. Along a temporal dimension, there are static and dynamic factors. Static factors are those that remain constant at different assessments, while dynamic factors are those requiring periodic monitoring for change. Within the context of this temporal dimension is a spatial dimension concerned with whether the focus of assessment is the individual (the offender) or his or her environment. Both individual and environmental factors may be related to past, current, and projected events or characteristics. Individual factors may be ascribed or acquired. These categories are not truly mutually exclusive; however, some factors potentially fall into either category, depending on one's theoretical framework. Ascribed characteristics are here defined as those with which a person is naturally endowed. Acquired characteristics here are viewed as those that are a combined function of naturally endowed dispositions and social influences. These may be objectively discerned (based on behavioural criteria) or more subjectively evaluated through psychodiagnostic techniques. Environmental factors affect an individual's development and his or her current behaviour (e.g. imminent influences upon parole) and relate to projected situational factors.

Both statistical and clinical assessments may include all the above categories of factors, although the former are more likely to place greater weight on the static than dynamic and a relatively balanced weight on individual and environmental factors; the latter, in formal terms at least, are reliant on more subtle and dynamic individual processes (Pfohl 1977). These dimensions of predictions are summarized in the figure.

Statistical and clinical prediction

There is considerable overlap between statistical and clinical predictive systems. The purest form of statistical device involves mathematical computations using archival data. Purely clinical predictions would be based on data obtained in the clinical examination. Statistical and clinical techniques can be combined when clinicians consider 'objective' biographical information and psychological test scores in their decisions or when clinical data are quantified and included in actuarial tables (Monahan 1981). The argument can be made that the two approaches are inseparable. In statistical prediction, many of the 'objective' data drawn from offender files, such as criminal history information, have been collected and recorded by human beings making considerable judgments and interpretations leading up to the decision to designate events as criminal. The clinician, too, while arguing that each case assessed is unique, can hardly contend that he or she does not compare the case at hand with previous ones and at least mentally place it in some subcategory or class. Undoubtedly, the clinician has some notion as to the likely outcome of the cases within a given class (Meehl 1954).

When the 'pure' statistical and clinical approaches are compared, several fundamental differences emerge. Statistical systems tend to be more explicit with respect to the predictor and criterion variables. Consequently, such schemes can more easily be validated. The clinician, when confronted by a differing second opinion, can contend that assessment is a dynamic process that cannot be replicated because of the idiosyncratic nature of each case at any point in time, as well as of the client-therapist relationship. Nevertheless, as Meehl (1954) points out, the use of statistics is unavoidable in the validation process, even in the case of clinical prediction. The honest clinician, he asserts, must at some point address the question of whether he is doing better in predicting behaviour than if he were to toss coins.

Aside from containing more explicit criteria for evaluation, statistical systems employ uniform criteria from one case to the next. Clinicians, in contrast, may consider the relevance of a criterion to a specific case (Monahan 1981). Further, clinical methods tend to involve a holistic approach, with a focus on the total personality. Specific traits are viewed in this context, and assessments comprise an intuitive aggregation of them

(Halleck 1967). Statistical schemes usually involve the additive compilation of specific factors (the weighting of factors is frequently involved) (Monahan 1981). This property indicates an assumption, in actuarial schemes, of the independent impact of these factors on the outcome variable.

Statistical devices are limited by the nature of the predictive statements they provide. By placing individuals in various categories of risk, they can indicate the percentage of successful outcomes in each group. Unfortunately, any particular case is either a success or a failure and each risk category is likely to have cases of both. Since members of the same group are to be treated equally in policy, errors inevitably result. Thus, even if statistical predictions are perfectly accurate, errors would still occur. If 75 per cent of those with a particular attribute were found to recidivate violently on release from an institution, the other 25 per cent of such persons would not manifest the behaviour of the modal group. Error is thus built into statistical systems. Clinical prediction, in contrast, can hypothetically be totally accurate if the assessment techniques and predictive indicators are perfectly reliable, although the general exclusion of ecological and situational variables places an upper bound on its accuracy.

Existing evidence indicates that statistical methods have superior predictive power (Meehl 1954; Sawyer 1966). Evidence of relatively successful clinical prediction does, nevertheless, exist (Kozol, Boucher, and Garofalo 1972) – although the issue of the base rates of violence or recidivism in general has frequently been ignored in such studies. Numerous studies have examined the accuracy of psychiatric assessments relating to offender dangerousness (Wiggins 1973). One recent study examined the extent to which these assessments met the criteria of expert judgment (Quinsey and Ambtman 1979). The four criteria considered were: 1 / clinicians agree with one another in their judgments; 2 / they are accurate in their judgments; 3 / differences in judgments exist when clinicians are compared to laypersons; and 4 / specialized assessment procedures are used. Clinicians were asked to rate a sample of patients. The study found that none of the four criteria of expert judgment was met.

Statistical tables, in contrast, are limited by their inability to consider cases that cannot be properly classified into existing categories. The idiosyncratic elements in some cases may be more relevant than the established criteria. In such an event, it may be useful to permit a clinician to override the predictions, as is done in the procedures set out by the United States Parole Commission (Gottfredson, Wilkins, and Hoffman 1978). A further limitation of statistical predictions is that they are more dependent then are clinical assessments on comprehensive biographical information relating to the offender. The information possessed by the criminal justice system, whether contained in police, judicial, or correctional files, is frequently incomplete, inaccurate, and ambiguous (Gottfredson, Wilkins, and Hoffman 1978). Also, in some situations, there is insufficient time to obtain the information necessary to complete actuarial tables. This may frequently be so with respect to the decision to release an individual on bail or in cases of emergency civil commitment (Monahan 1981). Recourse to either fixed legal criteria or clinical assessments may be required in such instances.

Static and dynamic prediction

Static prediction involves the use of indicators that remain constant over time. Such indicators can be historical (e.g. family history) or ascribed (e.g. race). Reliance on historical indicators can render an individual a 'slave of his past.' The problem with ascribed indicators is their questionable legality and the fact that they may only reflect discriminatory practices in criminal justice systems. With neither historical nor ascribed variables does the individual exercise current control over these factors, and he or she may become disillusioned by an inability to ameliorate his or her fate. The consequences for correctional officials charged with either the reform or custody of such people are clear. The repeated use of the same indicators in the determination of dispositions imposed on an offender may punish him or her again and again for the same acts or attributes (Wilkins in Monahan 1981). The use of static indicators is made attractive by their frequent availability in offender files and by the fact that such information need not be updated.

Dynamic indicators are those requiring periodic monitoring. Included here are such concerns as the psychiatric status of an individual at the time of assessment, general life situation, institutional adjustment, and even one ascribed variable, age. The state of Wisconsin, for example, requires that all probationers and parolees be reassessed at six-month intervals to determine whether reclassification is necessary with respect to custody (Baird, Heinz, and Bemus 1979). Such evaluations are geared towards examining the individual's present adjustment, as opposed to the criminal history factors emphasized in the original intake assessment. Of principal concern are such factors as the offender's adherence to the imposed conditions of probation and parole, exploitation of community resources, and ongoing interpersonal relations.

Although the periodic collection of information required by dynamic assessment is more costly and occasionally more difficult than that required for static assessment, it has the obvious advantage of outlining the current status of an individual. The crucial issue is whether dynamic factors, reflecting the most current information possessed by the criminal justice system, should, despite their constant evolution and inherent instability, have a weight in criminal justice decisions comparable to that of the historical factors that may have been responsible for the individual's initial misconduct. Undue reliance on dynamic factors would have the effect of diffusing responsibility for decision-making when the current trend is towards expanding legislative and judicial control (Fogel 1979). The use of factors based on the offender's 'evolution' towards a socially constructive role may lend itself to a multitude of abuses on the part of offenders and well-intentioned mental health personnel aiming to serve the offender's interests. An offender may arrange a marriage of convenience or play down personal or psychological problems if he or she knows that these conditions will lessen the sentence or make parole likely. Also, because dynamic factors are frequently subjective and 'measured' by clinical means, they lack the reliability of static indicators and thereby lead to an increase of discretion in criminal justice decision-making.

Individual and environmental indicators are subsumed within both static and dynamic predictive factors. In some cases, these indicators are the same for both approaches but are merely measured at different times. The factor of occupational status, for example, may be examined historically (e.g. the offender's employment history) or at the time of assessment (e.g. employment prospects). It is useful at this point to examine the means available to measure variables used in statistical prediction.

Measurement of predictor and criterion variables

To maximize the utility of predictive efforts, one must find the most accurate means of identifying those involved in criminality, the extent of that involvement, their individual characteristics, and the social or environmental context in which they reside and commit offences. There are four principal information-gathering methods to assist us in addressing these issues.

First, one can rely on the data collected by the criminal justice system: i.e. police, judicial, and correctional records. Such official crime data are the most accessible to the researcher, and hence it is not surprising that most empirical research in criminology has resorted to these information sources. Criminal justice data have, however, been criticized on a number of grounds (Hindelang 1976). Some crimes are never detected, and others are

not reported to the authorities or recorded by them. Changing legal definitions and law enforcement practices can profoundly affect the recorded
volume of crime, as well as the apparent characteristics of offenders. Also,
legal categorizations of offences are broad, and consequently different
types of behaviour may fall within the same category. The utility of criminal
justice data is also limited by the fact that official files do not contain information on many important aspects of a crime (e.g. the victim-offender relationship).

A second means of deriving information on the prevalence of crime, its
etiology, and offender characteristics is the self-report study. One can either
survey a specified group or sample within the general population or those
officially designated as offenders to identify those contravening the law, as
well as the extent and seriousness of the contraventions. It is generally
assumed that the self-report method will reveal a greater involvement in
crime on the part of a relevant sample than will official records, because of
its ability to probe undetected, unreported, and unrecorded crime. It also
provides a way to circumvent biases in the criminal justice system. Reaction
to self-report studies is nevertheless characterized by scepticism: one might
legitimately question the truthfulness of responses by those presumed to lie,
cheat, and steal (Hindelang, Hirschi, and Weis 1981). Also, the memories
of respondents may fail with respect to the nature or timing of their law-
breaking activities. Further, the instruments that have been used are varied
(Nettler 1978); they have been applied to many different sub-populations
and attained different degrees of reliability and validity (Hindelang,
Hirschi, and Weis 1981).

A third technique available to identify offenders and their characteristics
is the victim survey. It is even further removed from the crime itself, as victims are asked to recall information about the offender (Waller and Okihiro
1978). Such information is rather sketchy where the offender is a stranger
and non-existent where there is no tangible victim (in 'victimless' crimes or
those perpetrated against organizations). Victims, in some cases, may even
be unaware that a crime has been committed against them. For these and
other reasons, the National Crime Panel (1974) found that victims constitute a poor source of information on offender characteristics.

A fourth and potentially more enriching source of information is direct
observation of people in their natural environments (Farrington 1983). This
approach circumvents reliance on the accuracy of the criminal justice
system's data, as well as dependence on the truth of responses made by people about offences they may have committed or that may have been committed against them. Most studies in this category have been experimental,

with the investigator creating conditions favourable to the commission of deviant or criminal acts by the unwitting subjects. The costs and ethical dilemmas involved in such endeavours help explain why relatively few observational studies have been undertaken. Also, environmental manipulations by researchers bring into question the extent to which such work can be generalized. After all, the investigator is creating criminal opportunities that some subjects may not otherwise be exposed to in their lifetime.

The aforementioned four ways of determining the factors most clearly associated with criminal behaviour can be seen as complementing one another in an assessment of the leading predictive variables. The ensuing discussion of these variables therefore incorporate findings derived from all four methods. However, studies using criminal justice data are cited most frequently, reflecting their predominant role in criminological research.

Other data collection procedures are necessary when variables not directly observable are involved. Psychological tests and scales are available to probe the variables of intelligence and personality. Various medical tests and instruments are used to measure such factors as pulse rate, blood pressure, and neurological activity.

3

Individual factors in prediction

This chapter begins the discussion of the principal variables used in the statistical prediction of criminal behaviour and the mathematical techniques used to combine them. The focus of this work is traditional individual crime ('street crime'), rather than white-collar, political, or collective crime. As well, as has already been mentioned, predictions can concern an individual's initial involvement in crime or they can relate to his or her recidivism.

As Blumstein and Graddy (1982) note, the predictors involved in the two cases may be distinctly different. The factors that best predict criminality may also change over the course of a lifetime or criminal career (Loeber and Dishion 1983). Predictions of recidivism can be further distinguished on the basis of whether or not the crime involves violence. One can also aim to be more specific by predicting not only the recurrence of criminality but the frequency with which it recurs, the form it will take, and the context in which it will occur. Predictions can also be useful in assessing the likelihood that a person will abscond if released on bail, create disturbances in an institution, violate parole, or fail to respond to available correctional programs.

It is also recognized that the definitional context of crime may change over time and from one legal system to another. A form of behaviour that might be prohibited in one area may be permissible in another. Also, the manner in which offences are classified and the terms provided them may vary. In Canada's Criminal Code, homicide is broken down into first- and second-degree murder, manslaughter, and infanticide. Breaking and entering in Canada is equivalent to burglary in the United States. The discussion that follows encompasses a wide variety of predictive issues and contexts. Unless a point relates to prediction in general and applies to many different types of situations, the nature of the prediction and the context are specified.

The present chapter covers some of the leading individual-level predictors of criminality, in terms of both their predictive utility and their ethicality. The first section deals with what have been referred to here as 'ascribed' variables. One's status on these variables – sex, race, and age – is essentially fixed. The second section, dealing with 'acquired' variables, examines the value of, and ethical concerns relating to, predictive factors that can at least to some extent be modified (e.g. intelligence and social status).

Ascribed characteristics

SEX

One of the attributes most consistently related to criminal behaviour is sex. Cross-national evidence indicates that men are far more likely to engage in criminal activity than are women and that this imbalance becomes more pronounced with the increased gravity of criminal conduct (Dinitz 1981; Hartnagel 1978; Radzinowicz and King 1977; Walker 1965; West 1967). Victimization surveys and self-report studies tend to corroborate the findings from official data sources (Hindelang 1976; Hindelang, Hirschi, and Weis 1981). Virtually no observational work has been done in this area. Two Canadian field experiments conducted by this writer (Gabor et al 1986; Gabor and Barker 1985) revealed that female subjects were as dishonest as the males. One of these studies dealt with the inclination of convenience-store cashiers to return change when they were deliberately overpaid, and the other tested the responses of people to what they thought were lost letters. In both cases, the possible monetary gain by subjects was modest, and, as women are considered to be actively involved in petty theft, the findings from these studies should not be surprising or cast doubt on the existence of greater differences when more serious crimes are considered.

Sex-based differences may be underestimated when one considers the paternalism of criminal justice systems towards women, with the result that young women may be more likely than young men to be arrested for status and minor offences (Teilmann and Landry 1981). This is probably offset by chivalrous attitudes still existing towards adult women that result in a greater reluctance by law enforcement agencies to formally process women than men, thereby producing an underestimation of female crime in official statistics.

To be sure, a number of writers have suggested that sex differences in criminality are due to biological differences between men and women (Sykes 1956). The extent to which sex will remain a good predictor of involvement in criminality nevertheless appears, at least partly, to be a function of the female role in society. The continuing emancipation of women has contributed to a decline in the differential contribution of the sexes to crime as a whole (Adler 1975). The importance of the societal role of women is illustrated by the more modest differences in criminality among black men and women in the United States (Sykes 1956). This appears to reflect the more active participation of black women in subsistence-related activities. In Germany, during the Second World War, the gap in criminal activity between the sexes decreased when women were forced to assume major civilian responsibilities. Following the war, their criminality reverted to pre-war levels (Radzinowicz and King 1977). Also, a correlation between sex role differences and differential criminal activity can be observed in comparing different regions of the world. Asian and African countries, where women clearly play a subordinate role, tend to be characterized by substantially greater sex differences in criminality than occur in western European countries and North America (Conklin 1981).

Some feminists argue that criminally relevant sex differences will erode with the total emancipation of women (Adler 1975). Although the criminality of women is clearly influenced by their social status, the position that this is the sole basis for their more modest involvement in crime may be erroneous. First, the observed reduction of the sex differences in criminal activity accompanying the feminist movement may be explained partly by a decline in the double standards extending greater leniency to women in the criminal justice system (Radzinowicz and King 1977). Second, it is true that the proportional participation of women in some categories of crime has been increasing in industrialized societies, but among the more serious crimes, only in theft do they approach the absolute levels of men (Adams 1978; Conklin 1981). Third, along similar lines, the greater rate of increase for women in certain crimes is deceptive because of their exceedingly low levels in many of these crimes at the initial point of the trends observed (Crites 1976). Fourth, the feminist thesis of a new violent and aggressive female offender is not borne out by the evidence (Rita J. Simon 1975). Indeed, in the United States, there was a decline in the proportional female participation in both of the purely violent index crimes pertaining to women – murder and aggravated assault – between 1960 and 1973 (Conklin 1981). In Canada, between 1965 and 1975, women charged for violent index crimes increased only from eight to nine of every 100 persons charged (Adams

1978). There was no gradual pattern of increase during that decade. Indeed, female proportional involvement in violent crime actually declined from 1970 to 1975 (Adams 1978). Thus the increasing participation of women in some forms of crime must be viewed in the context of a decline, or at least a stabilization, in other forms. As Nagel and Hagan (1983) point out, the participation of women has increased in crimes traditionally committed by them. They have made few inroads into crimes traditionally committed by men. Finally, there is a question as to the role of feminism, as the observed increases have primarily been noted among lower-class women rather than those most actively endorsing feminist goals (Smart 1976).

Sex is still a good predictor of one's susceptibility to criminality. The extent to which this variable also discriminates well between recidivists and non-recidivists is in question because of the dearth of available data on the response of women to criminal justice system measures and the selective group of women to which available data relate. One thing, however, is certain. Sex differences in criminal behaviour vary across different racial, ethnic, age, and cultural groups – they are not constant. It is to the role of race and ethnicity in prediction that we now turn.

RACE AND ETHNICITY

To engage in open discussion on the relationship between race or ethnicity and crime is, as Radzinowicz and King (1977) have put it, 'to enter a minefield.' Speaking of tabooed subjects in criminology, Sagarin (1980, 18) has further asserted that 'one [the researcher] must be aware of the volatile nature of the material with which one is dealing, and the responsible criminologist offers findings with special care and circumspection when their potential for social harm is great.' Acknowledging these admonishments, we will proceed to plunge headlong into the minefield, but with full protective gear.

The factor of race, in the United States, is considered a good indicator of the prevalence of criminality in a region (Curtis 1976; Hamparian et al 1978; Wolfgang, Figlio, and Sellin 1972). More specifically, the black minority commits a markedly disproportionate number of street crimes relative to its numerical representation in the population. This is particularly noteworthy with reference to all four index violent offence categories (Silberman 1978). Indeed, in relation to similarly impoverished and persecuted groups, such as residents of Hispanic descent, blacks still maintain substantially higher per capita rates for both total and violent offences (Handlin 1962; Moses 1947; Silberman 1978). However, within the offender population, the difference in the extent of criminal activity across the races may not be as pronounced in terms of the rate of offending as it is in differentiating offenders and non-offenders (Gabor 1983; Hamparian et al 1978; Wolfgang, Figlio, and Sellin 1972). However, differential preferences in terms of crime selection and variation in offence gravity (blacks tend to commit more serious offences than whites) have still been shown to remain (Hamparian et al 1978; Wolfgang, Figlio, and Sellin 1972).

The debate rages regarding the basis for such differences. Some writers attribute them to racial oppression and the remnants of slavery (Silberman 1978), others to differential justice (Piliavin and Briar 1964), others to urbanization and social disruption (Handlin 1962), others to a subculture of violence (Wolfgang and Ferracuti 1967), and still others to outright racial inferiority (Gordon 1980). The hypothesis of differential justice deserves special attention because it raises the possibility that the racial differences in criminality assumed by most American scholars and subject to considerable theorizing do not, in fact, exist. Alternative measures of crime participation tend, however, to support the notion of black/white differences. Both victimization and self-report studies indicate the greater involvement of blacks, particularly in serious, personal crimes (Hindelang, Hirschi, and Weis 1981). Although the evidence drawn from the self-report data may be somewhat less clear, it has been observed that black men may be more likely to underreport their involvement in crimes known to have been committed by them (Hindelang, Hirschi, and Weis 1981). Thus, while blacks may face discrimination in the criminal justice system, this may at least partly be compensated for by their greater reluctance to report their participation in crime.

Focusing on the historical and cross-cultural experiences of the black, Jewish, and Irish peoples, Radzinowicz and King (1977) have attempted to gain a broad perspective of the problem. They begin with the proposition that racial purity is a myth, stating that approximately 40 per cent of blacks in the United States, for example, are at least half white and that many whites have black ancestry. Whereas, they proceed, American blacks account for a disproportionate number of serious offences, relative to the U.S. population as a whole, black immigrants in England from Commonwealth countries have, at least until very recently (Rutter and Giller 1983), been as law-abiding as native Britons except in relation to drug offences and prostitution. Their over-representation in these offences has been attributed to the particular characteristics of their culture of origin. In his comparative study of the North and Latin American systems of slavery, Elkins (1967) showed how the more closed and repressive system of the former elicited dependent, infantile reactions on the part of slaves. The assumption of such roles rendered the subsequent social transition to free status considerably more problematic than in Latin America, where slaves could maintain their ancestral customs and participate in commerce.

The Jewish experience, according to Radzinowicz and King (1977), has also varied across different cultural and historical contexts. In European societies in which Jews were deeply involved in commerce, as a result of their exclusion from the professions and land ownership, they were prone to commit primarily commercial offences and, for the most part, abstain from other types of crime. In societies where they were more integrated and worked as labourers, their offence patterns more closely resembled those of the general population. Moreover, in contemporary Israel, a great variation exists among subgroups of the Jewish population, with those of African origin, for example, being more actively involved in criminality than the Europeans. The key factor here again appears to be the unique sociocultural experiences of each subgroup.

As for the Irish, Radzinowicz and King assert that their domestic rates of criminality, except during periods marked by political violence, are substantially lower than either their urban or rural rates in England or Wales. They attribute this to the separation of the young migrant workers from their families and the difficult social adjustment involved in the transition from rural to urban life.

Another issue jeopardizing conclusions regarding differential racial propensities towards criminality concerns the different demographic characteristics of varying racial and ethnic groups. Calvin (1981) has argued, on the basis of 1976 U.S. population estimates, that whereas only about 24 per cent of all American males were below the age of 14, 48 per cent of poor black males were in that category. Given the assumed relationships between youth, poverty, and crime, the argument can be made that once these two factors are taken into account, racial differences disappear. This issue will now be explored.

AGE

Another ascribed variable considered to be a powerful predictor of criminality and often contained in correctional decision-making guidelines is that of age. The factor of age differs from those of sex, race, and ethnicity in one crucial respect – it is a dynamic variable in relation to which the status of all individuals changes.

The variable of age has attracted a considerable amount of controversy in recent years. Some writers, so convinced of the strength and invariance of the relationship between age and crime, have gone so far as to suggest that some of the stiffest penalties the criminal justice system can impose should be reserved for young offenders (Boland and Wilson 1978). Hirschi and Gottfredson (1983), still more recently, have shown that the potency of the age factor varies across different social groups. The discussion that follows should indicate the complexity of the issue and, consequently, the need to be prudent before we wholeheartedly embrace what has for so long been one of the least disputed criminological 'facts.'

The Gluecks (1937), in some of the earliest work, suggested that offender reform was frequently attributable to the ageing process and that the age of 35 was significant in the sense that only the most hardened individuals would persist in criminality beyond this point. Later, the Gluecks (1940) changed their emphasis from chronological development to that of maturation, asserting that a delinquent career, once begun, had to take its course. The implication was that an individual first engaging in criminality at an early age would mature earlier than one commencing later. A number of studies, however, indicate that the early onset of a delinquent career portends a longer and possibly more serious adult criminal career (Farrington 1983; Hamparian et al 1978; Shannon 1980; Wolfgang, Figlio, and Sellin 1972). Another phenomenon of relevance to the developmental process is the concept of the 'latecomer' to delinquency. Some individuals, though they are unquestionably in the minority, may begin their criminality in adulthood as the result of psychosocial stresses – including occupational or marital problems and psychophysiological deterioration (Cormier et al 1961 and 1964). Aside from these general notions regarding the onset and cessation of criminal careers is the idea, based partly on folklore, that a linear progression exists in such careers from initially frivolous offences to those of increasing gravity (Hamparian et al 1978).

A great deal of evidence exists on the international level with respect to both the disproportionate participation of the young (under 25 years of age) in crime and the progressive increase in this participation over the past several decades (Dinitz 1981; Mannheim 1965; West 1967). The latter development can, perhaps, largely be attributed to changing demographic characteristics of many regions. The baby boom following the Second World War resulted, by the early 1960s, in a dramatic increase in the youthful segment of the population in many countries. Underdeveloped countries, as a consequence of their continued high fertility rates, are particularly prone to continued increases in the proportion of crime by the young and, consequently, in the total number of offences these countries experience (Dinitz 1981). Similarly, particular groups within developed countries, by virtue of their high fertility rates relative to the general population, will continue to be over-represented in crime. Since such groups tend also to be more impoverished and 'crime-prone' than the norm, their contribution to overall crime can be expected to increase (Silberman 1978).

Sagi and Wellford (1968) have estimated that 30 to 50 per cent of the increase in crime rates in the United States from 1958 to 1964 is attributable to demographic changes alone. In an analysis of the age- and sex-specific criminal conviction rates of Canadian provinces and territories, Hartnagel (1978) found that men under 30 averaged approximately a sixfold greater conviction rate than those over 30, whereas for women, this ratio was approximately three to one. When the age and sex composition of the respective provinces and territories was controlled for, the risk ordering with respect to crime conviction rates was somewhat altered and the range of differences in these rates was narrowed.

Aside from the demographic thesis, the concurrent effects of modernization have been blamed for increases in the incidence of crime among the young (Radzinowicz and King 1977). Crucial factors identified in this respect are urbanization, loss of community control and familial cohesion, as well as an increased pervasiveness of moral laxity (West 1967).

Despite the current alarm over the rising criminal activity of youths, a disparity between the various age groups has long been acknowledged to exist. As early as 1833, the Belgian statistician Quetelet (1833) indicated that age was the most 'energetic' factor in the commencement in and desistance from crime. In a comprehensive review of cross-national data, Mannheim (1965) found the peak ages for criminal activity to fall between 14 and 15 years. The problem with the use of aggregate statistics is the possible confounding influence of various factors.

Most of the evidence stems from comparisons of arrest rates for the various age groups. That group with the highest crime rate is taken as the peak age for criminal activity. However, the rate at which offences are committed at a given age in a population indicates the incidence and not the prevalence of crime in that age group. Remaining unclear is the question of whether a small number of offenders are committing a great number of the offences or whether a larger proportion of a given age group is participating in criminal acts at a less intensive rate. When one compares rates at different age groups, the fall-off of the aggregate crime rate from one age to another may indicate one of the following: 1 / the desistance from crime on the part of a number of offenders by a certain age; 2 / the deintensification of criminality by a number of active offenders at a given age; 3 / a declining entry into crime of virgin (neophyte) offenders by a given age; and 4 / some combination of the above. Thus aggregated data do not address a major issue of interest with respect to prediction – whether the criminal activity of offenders is affected by the process of ageing.

A second problem in the use of aggregated data is that of cohort effects. An observed difference in the arrest rates of two age groups may reflect differential criminal propensities among the two birth cohorts being considered, rather than the varying susceptibility to crime of similar individuals at two stages of development. The more criminally active age group may be so because of unique criminogenic experiences shared in the development of its membership, rather than the age differential. According to Wilkins (1960), the birth cohort experiencing the Second World War at the vulnerable age of four or five would manifest increased crime-proneness and other disturbances as a result of the trauma incurred. Thus the age-specific crime rates in 1965 of 24- to 29-year olds (those born between 1936 and 1941) may be greater than those of 30- to 35-year olds (born between 1930 and 1935) owing to the trauma and other debilitating effects of war during their development, rather than as a result of differing age.

The method most appropriate in circumventing such problems of interpretation is the longitudinal birth cohort study, where the progression of a group of contemporaries is monitored through their development. Unfortunately, there is a serious dearth of such studies. In one major effort along these lines, Wolfgang, Figlio, and Sellin (1972) found, in their study of Philadelphia juvenile offenders, that the earlier the age of onset of a delinquent career, the more offences an individual is likely to commit by the age of majority (18). Further, a noticeable increase in the seriousness of offences occurred as the delinquent careers progressed. In a follow-up study, Wolfgang (1977) found, on the basis of interviews with chronic offenders in the cohort (those arrested at least five times), that between the ages of 14 and 17 they committed an average of four to five index crimes per year. Between the years 18 to 25, the rate of offending had declined to an average of just over three index offences per year.

In a self-report study conducted at the Rand Corporation in California, interviews with 49 career felons indicated that, as juveniles, these offenders committed more than twice as many serious crimes per month as they did as young adults and more than five times their rate as adults (Petersilia, Greenwood, and Lavin 1977). In another Rand study, based on questionnaires administered to 624 male California inmates, individual offence rates were once again found to decline with age (Peterson, Braiker, and Polich 1980). It was also found, however, that the younger the age of the criminal career's onset and the more serious and extensive the offender's juvenile crime record, the greater the likelihood that the offender remained criminally active as an adult. In an Ohio cohort study of juveniles conducted by Hamparian and her colleagues (1978), this was supported by evidence that the early age of delinquency onset is related positively to the number of offences committed by age 18. This is an expected relationship, however, by virtue alone of the longer periods of exposure of earlier starters to the possibility of criminal involvement and official detection. Further, since later starters were more likely to begin their careers with a violent offence and subsequently to be incarcerated, only minimal exposure time remained (prior to the age of 18) during which they could recidivate. The authors have found no support for the notion of an increasing gravity of offences with the progression of age. Indeed, of those engaging in their first offence before the age of 14, 59 per cent had at least temporarily desisted from a life of crime by the age of 17.

Shannon (1980), in his examination of three Wisconsin birth cohorts, also found the age of onset of a criminal career to be related to the probability of continuation. In the earliest birth cohort (1942), people with a police contact by the age of 13 (regardless of the number of such contacts) were certain to have at least one additional police contact following that age. In fact, well over half of these people had at least five additional contacts. As in the two cohort studies just cited, an early age of delinquency onset was positively related to the total number of contacts with the criminal justice system. An interesting finding was that individuals with four or more contacts prior to the age of 18 had a better-than-even likelihood of exceeding that number of contacts following the age of 18, whereas, for those with three or less prior contacts, the situation was reversed – that is, less than half exceeded their pre-18 total following that age. What this seems to indicate is an intensification of criminality for those already criminally active as juveniles and a tapering off for those never deeply committed to criminality.

However, several problems present themselves here. First, the time of exposure (years available to commit crimes) following the age of 18 exceeded that prior to it. Thus, an absolute increase in crimes following 18 years of age does not necessarily reflect an increase in the rate of offending. Second, dispositions involving incarceration may substantially alter this exposure time. If this time out of circulation is not taken into account, the velocity (rate) of criminal activity may be considerably underestimated. Since lengthy prison sentences are more likely to be provided an individual as his or her criminal career progresses, velocity at later ages may be greatly underestimated. If this is the case, Shannon's finding regarding an acceleration of criminality upon reaching adulthood, among those active as juveniles, may be further accentuated. Underscoring such a finding even more is the fact that none of the cohorts had reached the age of 40 at the time of the study, thereby presenting the possibility that some individuals would have committed still more offences as adults than those already recorded.

Age-specific crime rates based on time of exposure (controlling for disposition) in adult cohort studies have been obtained in only a few studies. Blumstein and Cohen (1979), for example, on the basis of four birth cohorts of Washington, DC, arrestees, found modestly increasing arrest rates for individuals in all the cohorts as they progressed from their early to late twenties.

Farrington (1983), reporting on an English longitudinal study that followed working-class boys up to at least the age of 25, found the peak age for both the prevalence and incidence of criminality to be 17 years. He also found a close association between juvenile and adult participation in crime. Of those convicted as juveniles, over 70 per cent were convicted as adults. Only about 16 per cent of those not convicted as juveniles were convicted as adults.

Another way of examining the age factor is to observe parole outcome at various ages. In a study of 7,245 parolees released in 1968 across the United States, Babst, Koval, and Neithercutt (1972) found that the probability of parole success was almost invariant across different age groups. This included comparisons between those aged 19 years and less with those over 40 years of age. However, when offenders were classified according to their prior criminal records and drug or alcohol involvement, those over 25 years of age consistently did better than those under that age. In a Canadian study of 423 Ontario parolees in 1968, Waller (1974), using the same cutting-off point of 25 years of age, found that the younger parolees were substantially higher recidivism risks than were those in the older categories.

Since much of the evidence of age differences in crime derives from arrest rates, it is important to consider the possibility that these age-related rates do not reflect the true criminal activity of the respective groups. Boland and Wilson (1978) claim that juvenile crime has been considerably underestimated by official figures. They state that the arrest of juveniles is less probable than that of adults because: 1 / their crimes tend to be less serious; 2 / they are more likely to select targets in their neighbourhood and are thus more often in a position to intimidate prospective witnesses from reporting offences; 3 / their offences are less often planned and thus infrequently tipped off to the police by informers; 4 / their identification by victims and witnesses may be made difficult by legal constraints that exist in many jurisdictions regarding the processing (fingerprinting, photographing, etc) of juveniles; 5 / they may be treated more leniently because of age; and 6 / juvenile records are frequently unavailable and/or are poorly maintained. A study by Greenwood, Petersilia, and Zimring (1980) indicates that this pattern does not necessarily hold nationwide, as jurisdictions differ greatly in their policies towards juveniles. In fact, they claim that juvenile crime may be overestimated because one offence frequently results in the arrest of several youths – a consequence of more criminal activity in groups (Zimring 1981).

The possible contamination occasioned by the criminal justice system's differential response to people of different ages can be overcome through using direct observational methods. In the two field experiments conducted by this writer relating to public honesty (Gabor et al 1986; Gabor and Barker 1985), people under 25 and 30 years of age, respectively, were found to be considerably more dishonest than those over these ages.

Aside from the varying volume of crime committed by the respective age groups, the issue of the differential gravity of misconduct needs to be addressed. It has conventionally been believed that an individual progresses from rather innocuous offences as a teen to more serious conduct as an adult (Hamparian et al 1978). Recent aggregated crime statistics indicate, however, that youths commit a fair share of violent and serious offences (Greenwood, Petersilia, and Zimring 1980). The general consensus appears to be that young teenagers are most likely to engage in less serious property offences and vandalism, those in their late teens and early adulthood are responsible for the highest proportion of serious property offences and violent crimes, while those in later adulthood tend to engage in more sophisticated offences (Dinitz 1981; Greenwood, Petersilia, and Zimring 1980; Mannheim 1965; Sykes 1956; West 1967), such as embezzlement, fraud, and certain sex offences.

Cohort studies provide inconsistent support for these notions. In the Philadelphia study of juvenile offenders, it was found that the likelihood of violent criminality increases with the progression of the individual from the pre-teens to late teens (Wolfgang, Figlio, and Sellin 1972). The likelihood of property offences was found to be less regular, fluctuating with the succession of years. In the follow-up to 30 years of age, it was found that the mean seriousness of offences increased steadily as offenders progressed from their juvenile years to early adulthood and then their twenties (Wolfgang 1977).

It is important to note, however, that this did not necessarily represent a simple progression of offenders towards ever more serious conduct. Based on a scale of offence seriousness constructed by Sellin and Wolfgang (1964), the seriousness scores of different age groups were compared. Although people between the ages of 13 and 17 had a considerably lower mean seriousness score than those between 26 and 30, the first group comprised 842 cases and the latter 239. It may be that the less serious offenders desisted from crime by the age of 26 and only the most hardened group remained active. If this is the case, two different groups of offenders were being compared, rather than the same group at different ages.

The Columbus, Ohio, juvenile study found that if an individual committed two violent offences there was less than an even chance that the second would be more serious than the first (Hamparian et al 1978). Few proceeded to subsequent violent offences. Indeed, when the delinquent careers were divided into thirds, the first arrest for violence was most likely to occur in the first third of the career and thereafter more likely to occur in the second third. The idea of a simple progression in gravity over age was again not borne out.

The value of ascribed characteristics as predictors, from both a pragmatic and ethical standpoint, is dependent on their resilience vis-à-vis the social context. If great cross-cultural variation exists in participation in crime by sex, race, ethnic group, and age, the forces of nurture rather than nature are, in all likelihood, the predominant factors underlying these patterns. If this is the case, the use of these factors in policy decisions may only serve to perpetuate the existing differences through self-fulfilling prophecies.

The manner in which criminological myths can be perpetuated is best illustrated through reference to one ascribed factor not yet discussed – physical attractiveness. Findings of two studies involving jury simulations indicate that both the probability of a guilty verdict and the severity of punishment upon such a verdict may be inversely related to a defendant's attractiveness (Efran 1974; Sigall and Ostrove 1975). It is clear that the physically attractive have numerous social and occupational advantages (Goffman 1963). In societies with a strong emphasis upon the physical form, those deemed unattractive or possessing deformities experience more discrimination at the legal and extra-legal levels. Hostile anti-social behaviour in response to such social devaluation has been clinically observed (Kurtzberg et al 1967; Lewis, Money, and Bobrow 1973; Zajac 1968). In one British study, three times as many facial disfigurements were found among offenders as in the general population (Masters and Greaves 1967).

Although alternative explanations can be advanced with respect to such findings, including that of offender life-styles, the implication is that the rejection confronting the unattractive may elicit anti-social behaviour which, in turn, reinforces such discrimination. Once an increased incidence of maladaptive behaviour is observed among the unattractive, they may be deemed to possess unique criminal propensities. At that point, policy-makers may intervene and legitimize societal responses that further 'validate' a relationship that, in reality, is entirely generated by social factors.

Acquired characteristics

Acquired characteristics are here defined as those attributes over which the individual may exercise some degree of control. The extent to which such control exists may be disputed on philosophical grounds. The distinction drawn between ascribed and acquired factors is meant only to reflect imprecisely this factor of control. The greater a person's control over a given attribute, the greater, perhaps, his responsibility for it. Also, the likelihood of both primary and secondary deviance (Lemert 1967) is diminished if the attribute and self-image in question can be shed by personal initiative.

Some relevant acquired factors include personality and intelligence, socioeconomic status, criminal history, a person's responses to previous sanctions, and alcohol or drug abuse. All these factors can be regarded in either a static or dynamic context, although differences exist in the extent to which they can be changed. Intelligence, for example, is generally considered to be fairly stable and rarely modifiable beyond 25 IQ points (Berelson and Steiner 1964). The use of drugs or alcohol, however, may be episodic, stimulated by stressful events (Kolb 1973), or merely affected by changes in supply. One may be interested in the personality, socioeconomic status, narcotic dependence, and criminality of the offender in the past or the effect of some of these factors on current or future behaviour.

PERSONALITY AND INTELLIGENCE

A large number of personality traits have been postulated to underlie criminality. These include psychopathy, inadequate personality (Eysenck 1964; Hare 1970; McCord and McCord 1964), various neuroses (Alexander and Healy 1935), psychoses (Zitrin et al 1976), and non-delusional disturbances in cognitive processes (Yochelson and Samenow 1976). However, serious mental disturbances are generally considered to be present in only a small proportion of offenders (Roth and Ervin 1971). Further, most psychiatric studies of offenders are conducted in an institutional environment. Such samples may not be representative of the general offender population, and psychopathology may be acquired as a result of institutionalization (McKay, Jayewardene, and Reedie 1979). As Monahan and Steadman (1983) assert, there is little, if any, connection between crime and mental disorder when the relevant controls are applied. Not only are just a small proportion of convicted offenders afflicted with some form of psychopathology, but the converse is true. The mentally ill are not more prone to violence than other persons, when prior contacts with the criminal justice system, social status, and other important correlates of violence are taken into account. As with the issue of intelligence and criminality, the effects of differential rates of apprehension, conviction and incarceration, socioeconomic status, and race must be disentangled from that of pathology. Thus, if those with psychiatric disturbances are more vulnerable to detection for their offences and less likely to have adequate legal representation, their disproportionate appearance among those convicted and incarcerated may be due to this ineptness rather than a direct result of the pathology itself. Moreover, the rates of disturbance among offenders must be related to the base rates for the population subgroup to which they belong, rather than to the population as a whole.

The literature on the clinical assessment of personality is replete with studies questioning the reliability of psychiatric diagnosis (Ash 1949; Pfohl 1977). Such problems may be due to differential psychiatric training, nosological difficulties, and substantive disagreements among clinicians. A major problem arises when psychological and behavioural variables are used to 'reinforce' one another. Guze (1976), when studying psychiatric disturbances among a group of offenders, found that approximately 75 per cent were sociopathic. The indicators of sociopathy he used included those of prior police contact, an assaultive history, and school delinquency. Thus this diagnosis of sociopathy was largely based on previous anti-social behaviour. In effect, then, a psychiatric condition was determined through behaviour and this condition was subsequently used to predict similar behaviour in the future. Such circularity has often compromised clinical predictions.

A 1950 evaluation of objective personality tests in which delinquents and non-delinquents were compared concluded that the results among studies were too inconsistent to indicate an association between various personality traits and criminality (Schuessler and Cressey 1950). One test, the Minnesota Multiphasic Personality Inventory (MMPI), which actually subsumes a series of distinct personality scales, has drawn particular attention in recent years. On the basis of the application of the MMPI to a sample of male federal inmates in the United States, Megargee and Bohn (1979) identified ten personality types and found an association between the extent of deviance of these types as indicated by the MMPI and their actual criminality. Although such results are promising, the possibility that this association is at least partly tautological needs to be considered. In their assessment of the MMPI's ability to distinguish criminals from non-criminals, Waldo and Dinitz (1967) found that the scale most consistently showing differences was the 'psychopathic deviate' scale. An examination of the items included in this scale indicates that some actually probe one's criminal involvement (Rutter and Giller 1983). An association between scale scores and criminal behaviour is therefore not surprising.

The issue of intelligence as a predictor of criminality is still the subject of considerable research. Contrary to earlier thinking on the subject (Vold 1958), IQ scores tend to be very strongly associated with delinquency (Hindelang, Hirschi, and Weis 1981; Rutter and Giller 1983).

A great deal of attention has recently focused on the biological bases of personality and criminal behaviour (Wilson and Herrnstein 1985). This resurgence of biological explanations is based on sources as diverse as studies of twins and adopted persons (Mednick and Volavka 1980), research involving the electrical stimulation of neural systems regulating aggression (Moyer 1979), some evidence that slow autonomic nervous system activity and recovery are related to criminality (particularly psychopathy) (Mednick and Volavka 1980), and observations that assaultive behaviour is associated with some forms of substance abuse (particularly alcohol and the amphetamines) (Amir 1971; Ellinwood 1971; Wolfgang 1958). Some of these studies, such as the work of Mednick, have been done with such sophistication and neutrality that they have gained widespread acceptance among social scientists and repaired the credibility problem produced by some of the early biological research in criminology.

Biological studies, nevertheless, tend to be compromised by at least one of the following problems. First, generalizations are sometimes made from animal studies where little experimentation with humans has taken place. Second, there are problems in measuring and defining some factors as electroencephalographic abnormalities (Mednick and Volavka 1980). Third, a great deal of naïveté prevails in the classification of offenders. Often all offenders in a study are placed in one of a few crude categories without regard to differences in their previous conduct and contextual factors in their offences. Fourth, biological anomalies may be acquired during development and may even result from a deviant life-style or confinement rather than be genetically based precursors of criminal behaviour. Since the samples of these studies often comprise institutionalized adult offenders, this problem of differentiating acquired from inherited anomalies becomes more pronounced.

Notwithstanding these methodological problems, the more credible current studies suggest a genetic basis to criminality (Rutter and Giller 1983). Farrington (1983) notes, however, that biogenetic variables stand a greater chance of being correlated with criminal behaviour simply because they can often be measured more precisely than socio-psychological variables. Overall, the evidence points to some genetic link with crime, although social factors still appear to play the preponderant role (Rutter and Giller 1983).

SOCIOECONOMIC STATUS

Socioeconomic status has long been considered a key factor in criminality (Vold 1979). Bonger (1916) asserted that capitalism brutalizes people (particularly the poor) through its encouragement of predatory behaviour and the limited opportunities it provides for the pursuit of legitimate activities. Merton (1968) contended that criminal behaviour is a response to a discrepancy between culturally defined goals and institutionalized means of attaining them. Thus, according to Merton, it is relative rather than purely objective deprivation that is crucial for people who do not have access to legitimate avenues to goals that they both desire and feel entitled to. Lower-class youths, frustrated by their inability to achieve high social status, according to Cohen (1955), invert the predominant value system to neutralize the potentially adverse psychological impact of their failure. Subsequently, Cohen indicates, they may join forces with equally affected youths, and the coalition thereby formed may serve mutually to reinforce their anti-social behaviour.

An alternative, although not necessarily mutually exclusive, position was that advanced by Miller (1958). He identified distinct lower-class values that are conducive to participation in criminal behaviour – this is related somewhat to the thesis of violent subcultures advanced by Wolfgang and Ferracuti (1967), although the latter's is a cross-cultural notion that is to some extent independent of social status. Whether one considers low socioeconomic status a direct antecedent to crime or as mediated by cultural or psychodynamic factors, the evidence concerning even this relation is less then conclusive.

Longitudinal studies examining crime rates during fluctuations in economic conditions provide contradictory findings regarding the role of absolute deprivation (Vold 1979). Studies in which the anticipated finding of a positive relationship between periods of economic depression and crime is obtained tend to conclude, quite expectedly, that the economic factor was responsible. Studies showing that periods of prosperity are marked by increases in crime tend to attribute this to such things as increasing criminal opportunities and declining family cohesion. Radzinowicz and King (1977) have shown that a near universal increase in crime rates since the Second World War (particularly in the 1960s and early 1970s) has been accompanied by a virtually ubiquitous (at least in the industrialized world) postwar improvement in objective standards of living. As for the thesis that such problems have been confined to capitalist countries, documentation by both Western scholars and official sources within Communist countries indicates otherwise (Conner 1972; Kalman 1981). In the United States, Wilson (1975) has cogently argued that in the 1960s, despite the longest period of sustained national prosperity since the Second World War, as well as the institution of innumerable programs designed to alleviate poverty and other forms of social deprivation, the rates of violent and other street crimes grew faster than at any time since the 1930s.

Ecological research has provided some of the strongest support for the postulated inverse association between social class and traditional crime. These studies have consistently found that the highest concentration of crime is in the central core of cities inhabited primarily by lower-income groups (Boggs 1965; Schmid 1960; Shaw and McKay 1942; Singh, Celinski, and Jayewardene 1980; White 1932). Included in many of these studies is the observation that exclusively commercial areas in the cities' core are highly vulnerable to crime, reflecting, perhaps, a sense of deprivation (Boggs 1965; Schmid 1960). The high burglary victimization rates of affluent households located close to lower-income areas also lend credence to this possibility, as does some evidence from interviews with offenders (Carter and Hill 1977; Hindelang 1976). A number of serious methodological problems jeopardize the validity of these studies and enhance the likelihood of 'ecological fallacies' (Robinson 1950).

Another source of support for a relationship between socioeconomic status and criminal activity derives from cohort studies such as those undertaken in Philadelphia and Columbus, Ohio. In the first, social class discriminated well between delinquents and non-delinquents when race was controlled (Wolfgang 1972). Individuals with low socioeconomic status (those residing in census tracts in which the median income of families was below the regional median) were found to have a higher rate of multiple offences and higher rates of recidivism and were more likely to engage in offences against the person than those of higher social status. In the Columbus study, 94 per cent of black violent offenders and 75 per cent of white violent offenders in the cohort were of low social status (using the same definition of social status) (Hamparian et al 1978). In the case of blacks, however, the proportion of violent offenders of low social status was not substantially higher than the proportion of blacks with low social status in Columbus as a whole. Also, in this study, a highly significant positive association was found between the poverty of a youth and his or her likelihood of recidivism.

The evidence regarding the predictive value of such factors as social status, race, and sex is characterized by one major problem. Persons with certain attributes (e.g. low social status) are generally considered to be more vulnerable to arrest, prosecution, and conviction than those with other attributes exhibiting similar conduct. The self-report study can be used here again to assess the rival hypotheses of class differences and discrimination.

On the basis of such studies, Gold (1970) contends that almost all youngsters have committed some form of delinquency and those who are caught constitute a small fraction of all offenders. Thus the distinction between delinquents and non-delinquents, he claims, is spurious – people can best be viewed on a continuum from more to less delinquent. However, many self-report instruments include questions about extremely minor infractions. The findings of self-report studies, taken together, do not illuminate the relation between social status and criminality. Some support the conventional wisdom, others refute it (Hindelang, Hirschi, and Weis 1981; Nettler 1978). In a close inspection of the findings that relate to the issue of class differences, Hindelang, Hirschi and Weis (1981) asserted that not only self-report studies, but also many studies using official data sources, show unconvincing evidence of a relationship between social class and criminality. This is particularly the case, they say, when one discounts the aggregate-level data drawn from ecological studies.

An additional way to study the relationship between objective socio-economic status and crime is to examine recidivism rates for persons of varying incomes preceding and following incarceration. A large number of studies indicate that pre-prison income level and job stability, as well as satisfying employment upon release, discriminate well between success and failure on parole (Monahan 1981).

The fact that the relationship between objective social status in crime is hazier than is generally believed raises the possibility that relative deprivation may play an important role in a more complex relationship. Relative deprivation involves a subjective feeling that, according to some standard, the opportunities available to an individual are insufficient to achieve that which he or she deserves. The standard may be a hypothetical conception of what is reasonable to expect, or, more concretely, it may be the status of other persons to whom the 'deprived' individual is exposed (either directly or through the mass media).

The fact that absolute deprivation is not consistently related to criminality, particularly in affluent societies, should not be surprising. Very few individuals suffer from acute deprivation of such intensity as to evoke a visceral response, through criminal behaviour, to ameliorate the situation. Hunger, the need for shelter, and other primary needs can most often be met more easily through legitimate means such as welfare and various charities. The selection of criminality to resolve this problem is usually an indication that factors other than sheer deprivation are at work. Moreover, only certain crimes can be linked to extreme deprivation – homicides, forcible rapes, and assault can be directly attributed to economically induced misery only by a fertile imagination. One would expect objects of crime more often to be necessary items or those convertible to cash than is actually the case. Observations of those confronting abject poverty have overwhelmingly yielded the conclusion that such people are too preoccupied by subsistence-related activity on a legitimate level, or resigned to despair, to become conscious of alternative courses of conduct that can rectify their situation (Zawadzki and Lazarsfeld 1935).

No less an economic determinist than Karl Marx acknowledged that the grievances of the working class are most profound when their objective standards of living are on an upswing (Marx and Engels 1955). This he attributed to the still more rapidly accelerating improvement in the life-style of the bourgeoisie which, in relative terms, actually reduced the worker's satisfaction from its level prior to the upswing. Davies (1962), in developing a formal theory of revolution, has contended that insurrections are most likely to occur when a prolonged period of social and economic development is followed by a sharp reversal, if only for a brief period. He viewed social expectations as rising at a similar rate as that of actual need satisfaction. When a sudden halt or retrogression in the improving objective situation occurs, an intolerable gap may develop between this situation and continued rising expectations, setting the revolution in motion.

Gurr (1968), in an examination of insurrections in 114 nations, concluded that relative deprivation, induced by either increasing expectations or decreasing opportunities, was the key factor underlying social unrest. He added that the greater the *absolute* intensity of expectations, the greater the anger when these are unfulfilled. In a study of 72 black-white race riots in the United States between 1933 and 1963, Lieberson and Silverman (1965) found, in a comparative analysis with control cities not experiencing the riots, that unrest was more likely to occur where the disparities in median income for the two races were least. Moreover, for the cities examined, black median income in the riot and non-riot cities was comparable, whereas white income tended to be lower in the former. Two factors may thus have been at work. First, whites may have reacted violently to their declining social status relative to blacks – despite such a reaction, they still were of higher objective status than blacks. Second, the rising expectations of blacks, due to their improved status relative to that of whites, may have stimulated a greater assertiveness on their part. Martinson (1972), speaking of prison violence, partly attributed its proliferation in the 1960s to the unmet expectations of inmates following rapid improvements in services and general institutional conditions.

At the psychological level, expectations are said to derive from prior experience that certain investments produce appropriate reinforcements or from observations of the rewards accrued by other persons making similar investments (reference groups) (Morrison 1971). Relative deprivation also is said to involve a perception that the attainment of these legitimate expectations will be blocked. Further, the probability of blockage (as perceived by the individual) must increase rather suddenly because a gradually increasing likelihood of blockage would prevent the legitimate expectations from reaching a critical level. The result is a cognitive dissonance or a perceived discrepancy between expectations and opportunities. This is introduced by either a sudden diminution of opportunities or the development of unrealistic expectations (Morrison 1971). Along with the discomfiting psychological state of dissonance are defence mechanisms aimed at reducing it (Festinger 1957). If these are not successful in neutralizing the dissonance, through lowering either expectations or the perceived likelihood of blockage, the deprivation will be viewed as social-structural and an outward expression of the grievance (perhaps violence) will constitute the dissonance-reducing mechanism (Morrison 1971).

The frequently ambivalent findings regarding the association between crime and economic conditions may, to some extent, be attributed to the different periods of observation – with some investigators focusing on the long-term trend of increasing prosperity and others assessing the economic conditions directly preceding observed trends in crime. Also, the effect of general societal economic conditions upon resources available to the criminal justice system must be considered. These resources are generally acknowledged to be dependent more on fiscal constraints than on the salience of the crime problem (Ernest T. Jones 1974). A prosperous economy would generally be more conducive to larger outlays for law enforcement. Increased police activity, in turn, may have a net effect of reducing crime if the deterrence yielded exceeds the additional criminality 'generated' (Ernest T. Jones 1973). Whatever the outcome, this intervening variable of criminal justice system expenditures may confound the relationship between economic conditions and crime.

The use of absolute or relative socioeconomic status indicators as a criminological predictor is problematic from both a pragmatic and ethical standpoint. Practically speaking, the identification of relative deprivation requires the measurement of subjective states. Objective social status, even if it were shown to be strongly associated with criminality, would present the policy-maker with the same dilemmas faced in the use of ascribed variables. The differential treatment of people in social policy according to their class membership could clearly result in serious social upheaval.

CRIMINAL HISTORY

Among the most fundamental canons of science is that historical events are recurrent and, therefore, reliable indicators of the future. Experience from diverse fields provides support for this notion. Studies of social systems under extreme stress from natural disasters, for example, indicate that the most crucial determinant of a system's response and recovery capability is its pre-disaster preparedness (Quarantelli and Dynes 1975). In the field of neuropathology, the psychiatric prognosis of brain trauma victims has been closely linked to their pre-morbid personality (Brooks 1974). In the criminological realm, the prior criminal record of an individual has generally been considered one of the most reliable predictors of future behaviour. Given the notoriously high recidivism rates plaguing the field and scepticism about the criminal justice system's ability to reform offenders, it is tempting to conclude that many offenders, are intractable and that, consequently, the best prediction that one can make is that an ex-offender will persist in his or her misconduct. The factor of prior record subsumes such considerations as the number and seriousness of prior offences, including violations of probation and parole, violence in and escapes from institutions, misbehaviour in the military, and so on.

The number of previous offences has been found in several cohort studies to be related (although not necessarily linearly) to subsequent criminality. Farrington (1983), in his British longitudinal study, found different factors to be predictive of delinquency and crime at different stages of development. Being rated as troublesome by teachers and peers was the factor most strongly correlated with conviction at ages 10–13. Factors such as daring, dishonesty, and having convicted parents were the most stongly correlated with convictions at ages 14–16, and having delinquent friends was the key factor correlated with convictions at ages 17–20. More potent than any of these factors was a conviction at the previous stage. Thus the best predictor of a conviction between 14 and 16 years of age was one between 10 and 13 years. This seems to suggest a pattern of continuity in behaviour.

In the Philadelphia cohort study of adult offenders (up to the age of 30), it was found that the probability of committing an offence increased steadily from 47.3 per cent for the first offence to 84.7 per cent for a sixth offence, given that the person had committed a fifth offence (Wolfgang 1977). Thereafter, the transitional probabilities of recidivism, up to the twentieth offence, generally fell between 80 and 90 per cent. Also, there was a general increasing likelihood that an offence was of the index variety from the first through the twentieth offence. This does not necessarily mean, however, that as an offender proceeds through his or her career he or she is progressively more likely to commit a serious offence. It may simply be that those committing more offences may have been committing serious offences all along, while the less serious offenders are dropping out of crime after only a few offences. However, it is unlikely that an offender could commit many index offences without being incarcerated for a prolonged period. It was also found that, when monitored at the age of 26, only 12 per cent of those without a juvenile record became adult offenders, whereas, 43 per cent of those with such a record continued their criminality into adulthood.

In the Ohio juvenile cohort study, there was no evidence of a progression towards the increasing seriousness of offences as individuals approached the age of majority (18) (Hamparian et al 1978). The pattern of offending that emerged resembled that of the Philadelphia group. A large number of offenders (29.5 per cent) were arrested only once, and a further 16.2 per cent desisted following their second arrest. Over 30 per cent committed five or more offences. Thus, here again, the predictability of recidivism after the first few offences is rather low, but becomes more certain thereafter.

Shannon (1980), in his Wisconsin cohort study, found a strong positive correlation between the number of police contacts a person has prior to the age of 18 and the number of adult contacts. He also found that those with the fewest contacts before 18 were still far more likely to commit a felony or major misdemeanour following that age than those without such contacts; however, the nature of the juvenile violation did not appear to make a difference with respect to the likelihood of serious offences during adulthood. Despite the improvement in the prediction of serious offences provided by a knowledge of the juvenile record, the best prediction that could be provided was that no individual would commit a serious offence in adulthood – this was due to the low base rate of violence.

The importance of the criminal history factor as a predictor can also be examined by observing the effect of a criminal record on the adjustment of people released on bail and parole. In a study of three different Pennsylvania samples of persons released on bail (1973–5), Ozanne, Wilson, and Gedney (1980) found criminal history to be one of the few factors to discriminate consistently between success and failure. In a Los Angeles study of those released on bail (1969–70), Gottfredson (1974) found prior offence variables to be central with respect to success. In the nationwide American study of parolees conducted by Babst, Koval, and Neithercutt (1972), a clear linear relationship emerged between the extent of the prior criminal record and parole outcome. Those with no criminal record prior to the one for which they had been imprisoned and paroled had a favourable outcome (one year following release) in 79.9 per cent of the cases; those with two or more prior sentences and either a probation or parole violation in their past had only a 50.2 per cent likelihood of success. In two studies involving matched pairs of burglary and robbery offenders released from California institutions in 1965, Jaman, Dickover, and Bennett (1972) found several prior record variables significantly related to outcome. For those incarcerated on robbery and burglary charges, the variables of age at first arrest, the presence of a juvenile record and commitment, a history of escapes from confinement, and institutional misbehaviour provided significant discrimination between the matched pairs with respect to outcome.

A Canadian study of the criminal cases of 802 offenders yielded the finding that social history variables are the best predictors of recidivism (Gendreau, Madden, and Leipciger 1980). Particularly important and relating to prior record was whether the individual had been to court by 16 years of age and whether he or she had recent drug offences. Waller (1974), in his Canadian sample of 423 parolees, found both the number of commitments to institutions and the seriousness of the most recent offence to be statistically significant predictors of outcome. Nuffield (1982), in her study of 2,500 men released on parole from Canadian federal penitentiaries between 1970 and 1972, found that in the prediction of both general and violent recidivism, criminal history variables such as the length of the offender's crime-free period prior to the most recent offence and the number of previous convictions, imprisonments, and escapes were among the most potent variables.

Studies relating the seriousness of the most recent offence to recidivism have consistently found that those committing offences against persons are substantially less likely to recidivate than those committing property crimes (Heilbrun, Knopf, and Brunner 1976; Neithercutt 1972). This has been said to be due to the impulsiveness of many violent offenders and their reaction to environmental stresses, as well as the greater commitment of property offenders to criminal life-styles (Heilbrun, Knopf, and Brunner 1976). The notion that more serious offenders are less prone to recidivism appears to contradict some of the aforementioned cohort studies, where a progression towards more serious conduct in a career was found and where those having committed serious offences in their teens were more likely to commit a serious offence during adulthood than those without such a prior offence. These ambivalent findings can, however, be reconciled in several ways.

First, the definitions of seriousness and violence differ across the various studies. Second, the cohort studies did yield the conclusion that the general base rates of violence are relatively low. Thus, there appears to be a large group of one-time violent offenders who commit 'crimes of passion' and subsequently desist from criminality (Gabor 1983). There are others who offend episodically, interspersed with long periods of apparently lawful behaviour (Cormier et al 1964). These cases would not be captured in most studies because the conventional criterion of successful adjustment is a lack of recidivism for two years or less after release. There may be, however, a number of violent habitual offenders who are as likely to recidivate as are property offenders. Indeed, were it not for the fact that many violent recidivists were incarcerated for prolonged periods, this tendency might become considerably more pronounced.

Closely related to, and to some extent correlated with, the length of an individual's criminal record is his or her velocity or rate of offending. The theoretical notion underlying velocity is that as an individual progresses from one offence to the next he or she becomes more deeply committed and habituated to a criminal life-style. This habituation is expected to result in the progressively increasing velocity of crime commission. Thus, the temporal intervals between crimes may provide clues concerning the tractability of offenders. Although few studies have examined this phenomenon, the results are suggestive of a habituation effect.

Cockett (1973), in England, examined the criminal histories of three different institutional samples of juveniles (96 boys in each) where all boys had at least four prior convictions without a custodial sentence. A steady increase in velocity (a decrease in intervals) was found, for all three samples, as the youths advanced from the first through their fifth offences. The three samples were then pooled and reclassified according to the age of the first offence. The first group comprised those who began their official careers in crime between 8 and 11 years of age; the second, those who began between 12 and 15; and the third, those beginning between 16 and 19. A statistically significant difference in the intervals between the first and the second offences was found among the three groups. Those with the earliest age of onset averaged 28.5 months between the first and second offences, the middle group averaged 17.5 months, and the oldest group averaged only 6.2 months between the first two offences.

For all these groups an increase in velocity occurred when this first interval was compared with that between the fourth and fifth offences. Thus, for the youngest group, the mean spacing between the fourth and fifth offences was 9.2 months, for the middle group this became 7.1 months, and for the group starting latest the mean velocity was 5.1 months. The decline for the first two groups was statistically significant, while the decline for the last group was clearly negligible. The significant decline for the two groups starting earliest can be explained by the extremely large gap between the first two offences for these boys – perhaps indicative of a tentativeness on the part of extremely young offenders. In contrast, the group starting latest experienced only a slight increase in velocity owing to the already high velocity after their first offence. It is interesting to note that the later starters maintained a substantially higher velocity throughout their careers. The author then examined the careers of 37 members of the group who had eight convictions prior to a custodial sentence. This group was subdivided into those beginning their recorded careers in crime between 8 and 12 years of age and those beginning between 13 and 17. A gradual increase of velocity was found for both groups up to the fifth offence, after which a levelling-off occurred. Here again, the most dramatic increase in the rate of offending was experienced by the group starting earlier – this was particularly evident following the second offence.

The most noteworthy problem in Cockett's British study is that of generalizability. In his effort to avoid the possible contaminating effect of dispositions upon his analysis of offence intervals, he selected for his sample only those individuals who had no prior institutional sentences but who, at the same time, had committed at least four previous offences. His analysis was thus probably restricted primarily to petty offenders.

A more recent study by Hamparian and her colleagues (1978) avoided this problem by including in the analysis all members of a birth cohort with more than one offence (the examination of intervals requires at least two offences) and subtracting institutional time served from the calendar time, for any interval, to obtain the time of exposure, or 'street time,' between offences. The findings, based on 572 juvenile offenders, closely corroborated those of Cockett. As in that study, a dramatic increase in velocity occurred after the second offence relative to the period following the first offence. This increase then continued more gradually until the sixth offence, at which time a levelling-off occurred. It will be recalled that this levelling-off occurred following the fifth offence in the British study.

When the intervals through the first five offences were averaged out and compared with velocity from the fifth through the tenth offence, the tenth through the fifteenth, and the fifteenth through the twenty-third, Hamparian and her associates continued to find gradually declining intervals from the earlier to later groups of offence pairs. Thus velocity appeared to be increasing as one moved from the first five offences (a mean of 10.4 months) to the subsequent five (5.47 months), and again as one moved from the tenth to the fifteenth offence (3.68 months), and once again from the fifteenth to the final offences (2.24 months). However, the ostensible increase may be at least partly attributed to the early desistance from crime by the low-velocity offenders and the persistence of high-velocity offenders, rather than simply the increasing velocity of a given group proceeding through their careers. Further supportive of the previous study was the finding that those commencing their careers later have higher velocities than those with earlier ages of onset. This may be an artefact arising from the confinement of the study to juvenile careers (up to 18 years of age). An individual beginning his career at 17 and having at least two offences can have only a high velocity.

The analysis of spacing between violent offences yielded the finding, once again, that velocity increased with each successive offence. Thus, the mean street time between the first and second violent offences was 18.55 months, between the second and third it was 14.48 months, and between the third and fourth it was 13.71 months. Again this apparently increasing velocity may be due to the high velocity of the most persistently violent offenders and the early desistance of the occasionally violent. As for the interval between the first arrest and first violent offence, Hamparian and her colleagues (1978) found that for those committing a violent offence after their first offence, approximately half committed a violent crime less than two years (street time) following their initial offence.

Wolfgang, Figlio, and Sellin (1972), in their Philadelphia juvenile birth

cohort study, found a similar pattern of increasing velocity during the progression of the juvenile criminal career. Across all offence types studied
(non-index, injury, theft, damage, and combination), dramatic reductions
in the interval between the second and third offences occurred (averaging
about 10 months) from that between the first and second offences (averaging about 17 months). For most offence categories, there was another major
decline in the interval following the third offence (averaging about eight
months). Generally, these declines continued up until approximately the
tenth offence, after which a levelling-off occurred. The intervals were computed on the basis of calendar time and therefore did not take into account
the time spent in institutions.

A different form of analysis of spacing has been performed by Gottfredson (1974) and Nuffield (1982). In an examination of variables relating to
the absconding of persons on bail in Los Angeles, Gottfredson found the interval between the current and most immediate prior offence to be of central importance. The lower this interval and, therefore, the higher the
velocity, the greater the likelihood that an individual would fail to appear in
court. Nuffield, in her Canadian study of parole, also found an inverse relationship between the length of this interval and the likelihood of recidivism.

The offender's criminal record is probably the most frequently used
criterion in criminal justice decision-making. A survey by the American
Justice Institute (Bohnstedt 1979) found that 92 per cent of 57 instruments
reviewed included the prior record as a decision criterion. Family and social
factors were included 88 per cent of the time, employment and education
factors in 81 per cent of the cases, a history of drug or alcohol use in 57 per
cent, residential stability in 48 per cent, and factors relating to the current
offence in 36 per cent of the cases. A prior record was considered in all 21 of
the pre-trial instruments reviewed, as well as in seven of ten sentencing and
parole release instruments, in three of seven institutional custody instruments and in 12 of the 21 community supervision instruments.

Criminal history, as a criterion in criminal justice decision-making, is
primarily a static factor on which an individual's status can only get worse,
but not improve. Monahan (1981) has argued that if an offender has been
punished for a crime, it is unfair, after a subsequent offence, to augment his
or her 'deserved' punishment on the basis of previous misconduct. This, it is
claimed, would be tantamount to punishing the person twice for the same
offence. However, von Hirsch (1976), a leading exponent of the 'just
deserts' position, insists that the notion of desert should include prior
misconduct. He further suggests that the time elapsing since the previous

conviction should be considered. The greater this interval, he argues, the more difficult it becomes to ascribe culpability for the current offence to factors relating to a prior offence. Moreover, von Hirsch adds that provision should be made for the expunging of criminal records relating to offences committed in the remote past. With respect to this issue, the Canadian Committee on Corrections Report (1969) recommended that, even for indictable offences, an offender's criminal record should be annulled after a five-year crime-free period following the last offence. Annulment in that context referred to the unavailability of prior record information to courts in sentencing decisions, rather than to physical destruction.

INSTITUTIONAL ADJUSTMENT

Little is known about the effect of prisons, but a great deal has been inferred from high recidivism rates, institutional violence, and episodes of psychopathology (e.g. the Ganser Syndrome). The effects of differing lengths, types, and degrees of confinement on different personalities and age groups have only infrequently been examined. One of the impediments to examining these effects is the disparate criteria for evaluating adjustment in different institutions. This is borne out by the American Justice Institute Survey of criminal justice system decision-making instruments in which institutional measures showed little consistency in the factors included (Bohnstedt 1979). This is mainly due to the largely subjective nature of these measures. The evidence that does exist suggests that institutional adjustment is a poor predictor of recidivism (Glaser 1964).

The traditional view of institutional adjustment associated with Clemmer (1940) was that of 'prisonization' or the gradual adoption by inmates of the values and attitudes of a presumed monolithic inmate subculture. It was postulated that the extent of prisonization was positively and linearly related to the length of time incarcerated (Zingraff 1975). Subsequently, this thesis was modified by Wheeler and others, who posited that a curvilinear relation exists in prison adjustment, whereby the offender's values are transformed from the pro-social values that he or she is assumed to carry into an institution, to anti-social values and attitudes in the middle of the term, and, finally, to pro-social values once again during the preparation for release (Hawkins 1976; Wheeler 1961). More recent work has indicated that adjustment patterns vary in relation to personality differences (McKay, Jayewardene, and Reedie 1979), the style of institutional management (Hawkins 1976), and subcultural traits 'imported' into institutions by inmates (Irwin 1970; Jacobs 1974). Thus institutional adjustment is currently believed to be largely influenced by conditions to which offenders are exposed prior to incarceration.

Given the lack of consistent and reliable data regarding institutional misbehaviour, perhaps the most appropriate way to examine the impact of confinement on subsequent behaviour and the prisonization hypothesis may be to examine the relationship between the length of prison time served and recidivism, controlling for antecedent conditions (factors imported into the institution) and such things as different management styles.

There have been several studies that have explored the effect of differential prison terms on parole outcome. Babst, Koval, and Neithercutt (1972) classified a national sample of almost 15,000 parolees (all incarcerated for burglary) on the basis of their prior record, age, and drug and alcohol use. For a number of offender types (there were 22 identified), less prison time portended a more favourable outcome than for those serving longer sentences. Unfortunately, for an approximately equal number of types the opposite was true. Taking the offenders as a whole, time served was not consistently related to parole outcome.

Jaman, Dickover, and Bennett (1972), drawing from a pool of California parolees, matched 75 pairs of robbery offenders and 120 pairs of burglary offenders on such factors as age, ethnic origin, prior record, narcotic history, and type of parole unit, varying only time served within each pair. Time served was dichotomized with one member of each pair having served less than the median time for robbery or burglary and the other having served more than the median time. Robbers serving less than the median time were found to have more favourable outcomes that those with above-median prison terms in all three follow-up periods (six months after release, one year, and two years). For the latter two periods, the differences in outcome were statistically significant. The same pattern held for the burglary offenders at all the follow-up periods, except that statistical significance was attained only when the groups were compared two years after release.

Beck and Hoffman (1976), in a study of 1,546 parolees from the federal system in 1970, found a slight, although non-significant, positive relationship between time served and the likelihood of recidivism or parole violation. The authors observed a general increase in unsuccessful outcomes for those serving the greatest amount of time relative to those serving a moderate amount of time within each of five offender groups classified according to risk. This latter group, in turn, tended to do worse than those serving the least amount of time. Waller (1974), on the basis of his Canadian sample of parolees, did not find the length of imprisonment to be related to outcome.

For juvenile offenders, Wolfgang, Figlio, and Sellin (1972) have accumulated some strong evidence pointing to the deleterious effect of incarceration in terms of enhancing both the likelihood and velocity of recidivism. They found that where a youngster started his career by committing an index offence, he was more likely to commit a second index offence, and considerably sooner, if he received a court rather than a remedial disposition. The type of disposition made little difference in terms of recidivism, where the second offence committed was non-index; however, here again a court disposition appeared to expedite recidivism by an average of over seven months. In those cases where an individual began his career with a non-index offence, the type of disposition made little difference with respect to the probability of recidivism to either an index or non-index offence. This may be attributable to the very small number of persons who received other than remedial dispositions. It could also be that the innocuousness of first-time non-index offenders overrode the potential adverse impact of a more severe penalty. Nevertheless, even here a court disposition was followed by a more rapid return to crime for both index and non-index recidivists.

Court dispositions were also more likely to be followed by recidivism after the second offence for the various combinations of index and non-index offences, but the sample sizes were not sufficiently large to draw any firm conclusions. Rather consistently, again, recidivism appeared to be expedited by this type of disposition as opposed to the remedial form. While the likelihood of recidivism after the third offence no longer appeared to be related to the disposition, the time intervals between the third and fourth offences indicate quite consistently that a court disposition was more rapidly followed by an offence than was a remedial disposition.

This general pattern of more rapid recidivism following court dispositions underestimated the actual situation, because many of those receiving court dispositions were incarcerated. Thus the true spacing between offences for these people started at the time of release from an institution, rather than at the time of the previous offence. The offence rate of these people, based on the time at risk, was thus even higher than that indicated by the calendar time length of the intervals between offences.

Hamparian and her colleagues (1978), in their Columbus juvenile cohort study, found substantial support for the notion that more intrusive forms of intervention may be counterproductive. Controlling for variables such as offence sequence number (whether the first, second, third offence, etc), offence type, age, race, sex, and socioeconomic status, they found that regardless of the offence sequence number, institutionalization tended to speed up recidivism (using street rather than calendar time data) and informal supervision to delay it the most. These two forms of intervention constituted the two extremes in terms of intrusiveness. The other two types of intervention examined were jail detention (the most instrusive measure next to institutionalization) and formal supervision (the third in order of intrusiveness). Across five different categories of offences (aggravated, robbery and other violent, assault and molesting, property, and status and public order), with no exceptions, the more intrusive the penalty the swifter the return to crime. Controlling for all the aforementioned variables and taking all offences together (first, second, third, etc), the average interval following an aggravated offence was 6.85 months for those institutionalized, 10.43 months for those jailed, 10.86 months for those subject to formal supervision, and 14.37 months for those provided informal supervision.

Although these five studies examining the effect of time served and the form of penal intervention have applied rigorous controls, a methodological caution is in order. Taken as a whole, they suggest that where the level of intervention is related to recidivism, the more intrusive forms adversely affect outcomes. Given the difficulties of control and randomization inherent in quasi-experimental studies, the possibility exists that a major factor(s) was not controlled for or that extraneous factors intervened. It is possible that those individuals provided the harshest penalties were a more hardened lot to begin with, and that the differences between them and the 'controls' were so subtle as to escape detection. These differences could involve highly intangible factors such as the extent of family support and personal demeanour (Frazier, Bock, and Henretta 1980). Studies already cited have indicated the importance of intangible factors in criminal justice decision-making. Perhaps such factors constitute better predictors of recidivism than the tangible ones generally controlled.

The use in criminal justice system decisions of either institutional adjustment factors or the mere fact that an individual has experienced incarceration is questionable from an ethical standpoint. The first lends itself to abuses from several sources. One source of data for gauging an offender's adjustment may be a clinical evaluation – a method fraught with subjectivity. 'Objective' indicators of prison adjustment, such as citations from correctional officers, have a limited meaning because of the lack of due process in institutions. Although grievance mechanisms exist, the ultimate arbiters of grievances are most frequently prison officials rather than impartial persons. Also, institutions are places where violent reactions are elicited on a routine basis and where an individual may be required to respond aggressively. The use of institutional maladjustment to rectify withholding parole or increasing subsequent sentences is ethically questionable because of the lawlessness and danger prevailing in prison environments. Penalization on such grounds may constitute a form of double jeopardy. Further, the use of institutional adjustment as a decision-making criterion invites play-acting on the part of the inmates. This latter objection applies to most dynamic factors, as the inmate and his or her collaborators (lawyers, family, and friends) can manipulate events to provide the most favourable impression prior to a decision. Fortunately, institutional behaviour has not generally been a key factor in parole or subsequent sentencing decisions (Bohnstedt 1979; Scott 1974).

A knowledge of the prior prison terms served by an individual has also occasionally been included in pre-trial and sentencing instruments. Even if such experiences are shown to have detrimental effects, the use of punishments incurred, in addition to past behaviour, in decision-making means that the offender is punished for what the criminal justice system did to him or her in the past.

DRUG OR ALCOHOL USE

Substance use and abuse may be related to criminality in several ways. First, it may produce biochemical, neurological, and related psychophysiological changes that may precipitate violent behaviour arising from perceptual distortions (e.g. the hallucinogens); agitation, hypersensitivity, and mood alteration (e.g. the amphetamines); or a lowering of inhibitions (e.g. alcohol) (Commission of Inquiry into the Non-Medical Use of Drugs 1973). These changes may involve a progressive deterioration of cerebral functioning (dementia), or they may be of an acute nature constituting a more immediate precipitant to, or facilitator of, violent episodes.

With respect to the precipitative effect, studies of the dynamics of violent offences have shown the frequent presence of alcohol not only for the offender, but occasionally for the victim as well (Amir 1971; Wolfgang 1958). Amphetamine intoxication has also been blamed for a smaller number of serious offences against the person (Ellinwood 1971). It has been argued that the incidents of violence in which these substances have been involved are a product not only of the abuse itself but, rather, the abuse by persons already predisposed to such behaviour (Blum 1969; Rubington 1969).

Second, the physical and social debilitation occasioned by substance abuse may lead an individual, out of economic want, to commit property offences. This type of behaviour is characteristic of 'skid-row' alcoholics (Commission of Inquiry into the Non-Medical Use of Drugs 1973). Third, dependence on a substance (particularly the opiates) may force the addict to commit property offences (including robbery) to support his or her habit. Such persons have been said to account for an inordinate number of offences. In a recent self-report study of 243 known opiate addicts in Baltimore, it was estimated that these persons had collectively amassed close to half a million crime-days – 24-hour periods during which they had committed at least one offence (Ball et al 1981).

Also, the use of illicit drugs or alcohol may make an individual susceptible to a criminogenic environment. The desire to obtain illicit substances requires that he or she enter into contact with unscrupulous persons and groups. The 'rip-off' in drug transactions has been said to account for a high percentage of drug-related violence (McBride 1981). Similarly, the desire to drink alcohol may involve patronizing neighbourhood bars, which are among the most frequent sites of violence (Bullock 1955; Engstad 1975). Whatever the nature of the connection between substance abuse and crime, a great deal of evidence exists to the effect that bail absconding and recidivism are, ceteris paribus, more likely to occur where such abuse exists (Babst, Koval, and Neithercutt 1972; Gendreau, Madden, and Liepciger 1980; Inciardi 1981; Jaman, Dickover, and Bennett 1972; Monahan 1981; Ozanne, Wilson, and Gedney 1980).

The inclusion of substance abuse among decision-making criteria in the criminal justice system is problematic. First, it is difficult to ascertain the specific quantities and types of drugs an offender has been or is using. The user, most frequently, is unaware of the specific chemicals and purity of the substances he or she is ingesting (Commission of Inquiry into the Non-Medical Use of Drugs 1973). Also, the effect of a drug varies according to such factors as dose, route of administration, personality, individual tolerance and fatigue levels, age, weight, sex, and general health (Merker 1968).

A great deal of caution must be exercised in using drug or alcohol abuse as a criterion for enhancing punitive interventions, despite the potent evidence that it may increase the likelihood that an affected person will be involved in crime and that one already so involved will become more criminally active. Being punitive towards the abusers of these substances indicates the adoption of a legalistic rather than a therapeutic approach towards this problem. The indications that the first approach has not been successful are overwhelming (Commission of Inquiry into the Non-Medical Use of Drugs 1973; Fattah 1977). Adopting the legalistic approach precludes the use of more therapeutic approaches to offset the potential delinquency of crime-prone individuals and the recidivism of others, as these persons will be reluctant to disclose their problems out of a fear of criminal proceedings.

4

Environmental factors in prediction

Frequently overlooked in criminological prediction efforts and policy is the environmental context in which the individual functions. These factors, as indicated in the figure on page 19 can be subdivided into the historical, current, and anticipated. Influences ranging from the family, peer, and general sociophysical environment to the availability of criminal targets, weapons, and mind-altering substances may have affected a person's past behaviour. In addition, one may need to assess the current status of these factors to determine their potential influences on, for example, an individual released on parole. More difficult, still, is the attempt to anticipate the status of these factors at more remote points in the future – this requires the specification of various contingencies that may arise. Monahan (1981, 129–30) has asserted:

With situational predictors, however, one must establish *both* a statistical relationship between a given situation and violent behavior, and the probability that the individual will, in fact, encounter that situation. One might, for example, predict with a high degree of accuracy that a given class of offenders will resort to violent behavior when confronted with a situation they interpret as a challenge to their masculinity. To predict the actual occurrence of violence, one would then have to perform a separate prediction concerning whether they will encounter such a situation during the period under investigation.

It can be argued that the inclusion of situational variables is the most pressing current need in the field of violence prediction. The principal factor inhibiting the development of situational predictors of violence is the lack of comprehensive ecological theories relating to the occurrence of violent behavior.

Aside from the differential time frames in which various environmental factors are operative – i.e. the past, present, and future – the manner in which they affect law-breaking can also distinguish these factors. On the one hand, an individual's family of origin may not exercise a direct effect on his or her criminal behaviour as an adult. This factor is more likely to predispose him or her to such conduct. The fruition of this tendency and the precise form the criminal behaviour will assume are more directly influenced by peer associations and the opportunity structures in the community (Cloward and Ohlin 1960; Cohen 1955; Miller 1958). More specifically, still, the time and location in which a given episode of behaviour occurs will be directly influenced by physical aspects of environments that can inhibit or facilitate an act – surveillance levels in an area, the prevalence of crime prevention technologies, weapons, drugs or alcohol, and the accessibility of such dangerous sites as bars.

Environmental factors can thus be distinguished on the basis of their remoteness from the criminal act itself. Remoteness, in this sense, is in no way meant to reflect the importance of a given factor in the causal sequence culminating in criminal behaviour. Rather, it refers to the location of the factor in that sequence. In terms of elapsed time, a more 'remote' factor need not have exerted an influence long before situational facilitators. Indeed, the influence of the two factors may be simultaneous and interactive.

A good example of the interaction of differentially remote factors is provided by containment theory (Reckless 1961). The family environment, according to this perspective, is viewed as potentially inhibiting criminal behaviour through the instillment of a strong self-concept and pro-social values. However, subcultural pressures may be pulling the individual in the opposite direction. These pressures will be continuously interacting, with the net result based on the relative strength of the containment versus the pull factor. It is conceivable that neither of the factors will totally prevail, as the individual may drift in and out of criminality (Cormier et al 1964; Matza 1966), may desist after briefly flirting with delinquency (Hamparian et al 1978), or may commit the first act of criminality in adulthood (Cormier et al 1961).

Aside from the differential location of environmental factors in the sequence of events leading up to a crime, the same factor may operate at various levels of remoteness to the criminal conduct. The peer environment to which an individual is exposed, for example, may itself serve as a primary socializing agent, instilling self-discipline and providing emotional support (James B. Jacobs 1974). At the same time, it will perform its conventional role of transmitting subcultural values and, perhaps, rationalizations and skills required in criminal behaviour. On still another level, the peer group may introduce the individual to drugs, facilitate the acquisition of weapons, or actually coerce or prod the individual into undertaking criminal actions.

Thus the role of the peer environment may relate directly to the actual criminal act itself (its timing, location, and the form it assumes), as well as nurture the propensity to behave in an unlawful manner.

An environmental factor may thus play a single or more highly complex role in crime. In the brief section to follow, some evidence is introduced regarding the predictive utility of family and peer environments, as well as ecological factors generally more directly affecting the criminal act itself.

Family environment

Since the work of the Gluecks, a great deal of evidence has been accumulated regarding the integral role of the family with respect to criminality; specifically, such factors as family cohesiveness, as well as parental separation, affection, discipline, aggression, and consistency (Glueck and Glueck 1950; Moos 1975). An additional large number of studies document the important bearing of family settings upon recidivism for probationers and persons released from confinement (Moos 1975). There is a dearth of evidence comparing the relative predictive power of family environment variables (whether the family of origin or procreation) with others, such as criminal history variables. Most studies merely include such information as the marital status of an individual, rather than that concerning the characteristics of the family milieu. Where evidence does exist, regardless of the specificity of family-related data, this dimension has consistently been found to be of secondary importance to ascriptive and criminal history variables (Gendreau, Madden, and Leipciger 1980; Jaman, Dickover, and Bennett 1972; Ozanne, Wilson, and Gedney 1980).

One observation buttressing the notion of a pivotal family role in crime relates to the existence of the multi-delinquent family in which several siblings and/or generations have been at odds with the law. A classic study, in this respect, was that undertaken by Dugdale (1877) in which he outlined the depravity of the Jukes family. A recent media account reported a story of a California family in which all three generations are criminally active and have amassed 400 arrests in the past ten years (*Newsweek* 1981). Cormier (1965), in a study of 50 multi-delinquent families, found that of 249 sons produced, 149 were known delinquents (117 of whom had served at least one penitentiary sentence). Reckless and Dinitz (1972) have stated that over half of the juvenile court cases in the typical American city derive from multi-problem families, even though such families constitute only 7 to 10 per cent of all urban families.

The family, aside from contributing to criminality through heredity, psychopathology, and the transmission of anti-social values, may precipitate violence in a more direct fashion. Since the pivotal study of homicide by Wolfgang (1958), the home has been recognized as among the most frequent sites of violence. In the case of domestic homicide, the relation between the assailant and victim has frequently degenerated to such an extent that situational contingencies such as the availability of weapons and the likelihood of arrest are probably secondary to the impassioned feelings existing prior to the act. This is illustrated by the diverse forms of weapons and 'M-O' used in such cases (Wolfgang 1958).

Peer environment

The peer environment may affect behaviour through its role of primary socializing agent or that of situational facilitator. An extensive literature points to the central role of the peer group in criminality (Martin and Fitzpatrick 1964); however, quantitative evidence comparing the importance of peer influence and other factors is quite scarce. The evidence that does exist indicates that there is a positive correlation between the number of officially delinquent friends one has and the number of offences one will commit (Hindelang, Hirschi, and Weis 1981). The proportion of crimes committed with accomplices further supports the primacy of the peer group in crime. Group crimes are most likely to be committed by young offenders and are most likely to occur in the case of armed robbery and related offences (Zimring 1981; Gabor and Gottheil 1984). Moreover, there is some evidence that gang membership will increase the number and seriousness of offences an offender will commit (Wolfgang 1985).

Another indication of the potency of the peer environment is the recent documentation of the penetration of neighbourhood gangs into the American correctional system. The resulting polarization of inmates along racial, ethnic, and political lines has led some observers of prison life to discard notions of a monolithic inmate society and a uniform code of conduct. Various gangs have shown a continuity from the street to institutions – with the gangs' organization, formal and informal rules, and rituals being maintained. As James B. Jacobs (1974) has noted, such gangs may circulate their own written codes for institutional conduct to incoming members. These gangs provide protection and emotional support as well as facilitating the acquisition of contraband for their membership.

Situational factors

The situational perspective has ascended to a prominent role in criminology in recent years (Clarke 1983). This perspective is concerned with the situations one may encounter in everyday life that may enhance the likelihood of criminal conduct. One's exposure to criminogenic situations is not random but related to such factors as one's social status, as these situations tend to proliferate in those areas with more profound social problems. These factors include:

1 *The socio-demographic characteristics of the area in which an individual resides and otherwise spends a large proportion of time.* If such a neighbourhood contains a high percentage of people deeply involved in crime, serious economic problems, prevalent drug or alcohol abuse, and related social ills, the likelihood of an individual's initial involvement or relapse into crime, irrespective of personal characteristics, would tend to be greater than in a more socially stable and prosperous neighbourhood (Jeffery 1977). In such areas, the individual would be more likely to encounter pressures, temptations, and values conducive to anti-social behaviour. As well, in communities in which crime is rampant, the individual is more likely to encounter threatening situations in which violent retaliation is necessary and, perhaps, expected. Wolfgang (1985) has reported that victimization is frequently an antecedent of criminal behaviour: a person who has been previously victimized by a criminal offence is more likely to become an offender than one who was not so victimized.

2 *The frequenting of particularly dangerous sites within these neighbourhoods.* Areas with large transient populations, containing rooming-houses and a large number of bars, have been found to be sites of a disproportionate number of violent, public order, and vice-related offences (Bullock 1955; Engstad 1975). Similarly, parks, bus terminals, and related sites in urban areas, with their transient populations, illicit transactions, and physical design, may render the individual more vulnerable (Jeffery 1977).

3 *Criminal opportunities in a given area relative to the threat of detection by members of the public or police.* Such factors as the availability of desired targets (Engstad 1975), the availability of weapons (Monahan 1981), surveillance levels in an area (including pedestrian and vehicular traffic, vegetation obstructive to visibility, the employment of defensible space concepts, occupancy rates in homes, and street lighting) (Clarke and Mayhew 1980; Jacobs 1961; Jeffery 1977; Luedtke and Associates 1970; Newman 1972; Reppetto 1974; Tyrpak 1975), the existence of alarm systems and other crime prevention technologies (Kornblum 1979; Luedtke and Associates 1970; Reppetto 1974), and police or citizen patrol practices may all play a role in the individual's decision to commit unlawful behaviour and

the selection of the type, time, and location, as well as the frequency, of such behaviour. It may be argued that the extent of criminal opportunity is irrelevant because its curtailment will not inhibit the criminal activity of one predisposed to such behaviour but will merely displace behaviour in such a manner as to circumvent existing obstacles (Gabor 1981). The evidence relating to such a claim is as yet far too preliminary for definitive statements on this matter. However, total displacements of criminal activity (i.e. where the volume of displaced crime equals that which was suppressed) have not been observed (Gabor 1978; Reppetto 1976).

4 *Territoriality and population density.* It has been hypothesized that offenders (particularly the violent) have lower anxiety thresholds when their personal space is infringed. In spatial terms, this means that some individuals routinely require more personal space to function without anxiety. Upon infringement of this 'body buffer zone,' the person may behave aggressively. Ambivalent evidence exists as to the reality of these differences between violent offenders and others (Wilds 1973).

A more commonly presumed relationship is that between population density and crime. It has been believed that excessive crowding is a major contributing factor to high crime rates in congested urban areas. In fact, most studies controlling the often-confounding effects of ethnicity and social class indicate that no such relationship exists, whether it is the density of a neighbourhood or of housing arrangements that is considered (Freedman 1975; Gabor and McFarlane 1982).

It has also been claimed that overcrowding is a primary factor underlying prison disturbances (Cohen, Cole, and Bailey 1976). However, this has not been substantiated through studies in which the characteristics of prison inmates, level of security, managerial style, and general institutional conditions have been controlled. It may be possible that density in a civilian population is unrelated to aggression, whereas such a relation does obtain in an institutional setting. Such a finding could be explained by several factors. First, it could be that density must reach a certain threshold before its adverse effects are experienced. This threshold may be achieved only in correctional and other total institutions. Another important factor is the time of exposure to given densities (Freedman 1975). The civilian, even in a major metropolitan area, is rarely exposed to high-density situations for the duration of an entire day. The civilian may exercise various options to obtain relief from overcrowding (e.g. a stroll in a park or on a quiet street). Confinement in a correctional institution, due to its around-the-clock nature, the regimented and collective nature of activities, the perpetual noise, and the lack of privacy for even bodily functions, is a more encompassing and intense experience. Finally, density may be relevant to prisoners but not civilians, precisely because the former constitute a more aggressive lot from the outset. Thus, some offenders may be more sensitive to over-crowding owing to their requirements of larger buffer zones, as well as other factors.

5 *The availability of drugs and alcohol.* As elaborated in the previous section, knowledge that an individual with prior drug problems has ready access to such substances will surely lessen his or her chances of parole success. The likelihood of physical debilitation and subsequent inability to work, the inordinate funds that may be required to support a drug habit, the unscrupulous persons with whom he or she may enter into contact, and the possible direct criminogenic effects of the substances themselves all militate against success.

These and other situational/environmental factors are not, in reality, mutually exclusive or additive influences upon behaviour. A problematic family environment and simultaneous drug-taking may provide a poorer prognosis for the individual than merely the sum total of their independent effects. In addition, similar circumstances may elicit a diversity of reactions from different people. Further, as Toch (1980) has shown in his study of violence-prone individuals, people frequently choose to enter or create dangerous situations or environments. Personality and situational factors must thus be viewed together.

In considering the use of environmental factors in prediction, it is important, from an ethical standpoint, to differentiate those factors over which an individual exercises no control (or at least current control) from those that he can readily alter. The characteristics of an individual's family of origin can no more be modified than his or her age or race, and, thus, all objections pertaining to ascribed variables are applicable to static or historical environmental factors. However, decisions to frequent bars that are often the sites of violence, to engage in illicit drug transactions, and to carry lethal weapons are more amenable to change. Somewhere between these two extremes are such factors as area of residence, where the individual is physically free to change environments although perhaps prevented from so doing by financial constraints, familial considerations, and the like.

One further point that should be made regarding the use of dynamic environmental variables is that their use can lend themselves to abuse and deception by offenders. If family stability is considered a good predictor of parole success and is explicitly used in parole decisions, the individual can misrepresent facts about his or her family to create a semblance of stability.

Intuitive prediction

As we have said, prediction in some form inheres in all human behaviour, including decision-making at all levels of criminal justice systems. Thus, the decision by a police officer to arrest a juvenile may be governed partly by his projection of a youth's past behaviour and attributes into the future. Youngsters with a certain history and/or attributes may be more prone to arrest because the officer involved feels the youth is intractable and 'will never amount to anything.' Judges also may make intuitive predictions about an accused that may affect a disposition. These intuitive predictions may operate at varying levels of awareness. Their impact upon the ultimate decision is difficult to discern because they are so intertwined with other factors, such as the philosophical position of the decision-maker and the facts of the case. The former will dictate the importance of predictions relative to other criminal justice objectives. Intuitive predictions may influence perceptions of the facts of a case rather than simply be based on them.

One of the most notable experiments in intuitive prediction was the Cambridge-Somerville Youth Project, where teachers and policemen were asked to nominate pre-adolescents who were likely to have future difficulties with the law (Powers and Witmer 1951). Predictions were based on these nominations, as well as on assessments made by three clinicians. Matched pairs of subjects were allocated to experimental and control groups, with the first receiving intensive counselling and other forms of intervention, while the control group was withheld such treatment. A follow-up two decades later, arrived at the well-known conclusion that serious prediction errors occurred and that the treatment regime was generally ineffective. Indeed, false positives outnumbered true positives by a ratio of approximately three to two. This ratio may be somewhat inflated if one considers the possibility that some youths participated in delinquent behaviour that was never detected. Another important point to note is that predictions made for the boys from the more delinquent neighbourhoods contained far fewer false positives than those for boys from better neighbourhoods. This was due to the greater base rates of delinquency in such areas. Finally, as is rarely pointed out, very few false negative errors occurred – despite the high base rates of delinquency in the entire group. There were over seven correct predictions of non-delinquency for every incorrect prediction. In the study as a whole, correct predictions outnumbered errors by a slight margin. Although this study has been considered a classic example of the flaws inherent in prediction, the findings are not radically different from those of more systematic, actuarial efforts.

A more successful effort in intuitive prediction has been observed in Columbus, Ohio (Reckless and Dinitz 1972). There, a number of schools in high delinquency areas were visited and sixth-grade teachers asked to nominate both students who were unlikely to become delinquent (designated as the good boys) and those possibly or likely to get into trouble (the bad boys). The predicted 'bad' boys were then divided into experimental and control groups, with the former being provided a special program to boost their self-concepts – as this factor was seen as possibly differentiating the good from the bad boys. The control group was withheld any such intervention, and the good boys served as a comparison group. Prior to the program, about 20 per cent of the bad boys and 5 per cent of the good boys were known to the police. If the teachers were generally unaware of the legal status of the students, these figures are already indicative of their ability to discriminate the good from the bad boys. Assuming this to be the case, the teachers' nominations also proved to discriminate quite well between good and bad boy delinquent behaviour following (for a three-year period) the program. During the program, the predicted bad boys were six times as likely as the good boys to get into trouble. In the follow-up period, the bad boys were two and one-half times as likely to have police contacts. This reduction in the differences between the two groups cannot be attributed to the program, as negligible differences were found between the experimental and control groups either during or following the program. It appears that aside from the overall difference in delinquency between the good and bad boys, a higher proportion of the good boys embarked upon their delinquent careers at a later age.

Another study involving teachers' predictions was a retrospective analysis in Kansas City of the classroom personality and behaviour of 104 delinquents in their early school years (Khleif 1964). The end-of-year reports on these delinquents' personality and behaviour, provided by teachers for the first five years of school, were compared with a matched group of controls. It was found that those ultimately to become delinquent were more than twice as often cited for misconduct, almost twice as often for having an 'objectionable personality,' almost twice as often for having poor work habits, and more than twice as often for having a poor attitude towards school than were the non-delinquents.

5

Statistical methods in prediction

Once the variables have been selected for a statistical predictive effort, decisions must be made regarding the manner in which these should be combined to meet the objectives of prediction. First and foremost of these objectives, of course, is that of maximizing the predictive ability or power of the variables in question; or, put conversely, the minimization of predictive errors, be these false positives or negatives. Put another way, the predictive power of a variable or set of variables is their ability to discriminate between various outcomes. Thus, in a criminological context, a parole board would be interested in the risk an offender poses to society, in the event he or she is granted a release. Let us suppose the board wished to predict whether a person would recidivate within a specified period after release. Let us also suppose that they felt that a person's criminal history is the best predictor of recidivism. They might arbitrarily decide, for example, to release those with no prior record or with one previous offence and deny parole to those with two or more prior offences. The predictive power of the prior criminal record could be examined by looking at the outcome of a number of cases. The accompanying table represents a hypothetical group of offenders who have been followed up upon their release from prison and whose prior criminal activity has been noted.

Presuming that a sufficient sample of offenders, representative of the varying degrees of a criminal record, has been drawn, we can immediately state that there is some association (an inverse one) between the number of recorded offences one has and the likelihood of success after release from an institution. There is a consistent decline in the proportion of successes from the category possessing no criminal record prior to the offence for which they have been incarcerated to those possessing over four prior offences. However, the extent of the decline in the rate of successes is not

The relation between prior record and success
upon release from prison

Previous offences	Percentage successful
0	80
1	56
2	38
3	32
4	24
5 and over	20

equal when different groups are compared. There is a noticeable difference in the success rate between those with no prior offences and those with only one (80 per cent and 56 per cent, respectively). There is also a major drop in successes when one compares those with one and two previous offences (56 per cent and 38 per cent, respectively). The table indicates that the differences in success rate diminish as one compares the groups with longer criminal records. This finding would suggest that once people have three recorded offences, they are a high recidivism risk and that there is no appreciable difference between them and those who have chalked up a far more extensive record. A logical distinction on the part of a parole board, on the basis of this table, might be threefold: those with no prior offences might constitute a low-risk category, those with one previous offence a medium-risk category, and those with two or more previous offences, a high-risk category.

This type of classification would be more powerful as there are marked differences in the success rates of these three groups. However, using the prior record as categorized in the table as a predictor of recidivism is less powerful because some of the categories are virtually redundant. From a policy standpoint, it is meaningless to distinguish those with four prior offences from those with five or more, as the success rate is almost identical for the two groups. The more different the categories are from one another in terms of a success rate, the more powerful a predictor the relevant variable (in this case prior record) is.

A variety of statistical measures exist to determine the power of a predictive model. In this case, one can apply a test of independence such as chi-square to see whether the success or failure rates are significantly different across the various groups that have been formed by classifying offenders according to the number of their previous offences. The various measures of predictive power, as well as their respective strengths and deficiencies, have already been discussed in detail by Frances H. Simon (1971) and, consequently, will not be treated here.

The power of a predictive model can, of course, be enhanced by adding more variables, providing they are able to reclassify offenders in such a way as to improve the model's discrimination between the various categories of the outcome variable (in our case, successes and failures on release from prison).

The effectiveness of a predictive model, however, must be tempered by the consideration of efficiency. The development of parsimonious predictive schemes is important for several reasons. First, the fewer variables that are included, the less expensive it is for the criminal justice system to collect the information necessary for the initial development of a predictive instrument. Second, the updating of a predictive instrument (this should be an ongoing process) (Ohlin 1951) requires a sample proportional to the number of variable used. Large numbers of variables require samples of enormous magnitude to make statistical inferences or else cell counts will be too small. Third, the practitioner using the device will need to obtain all information required on a case-by-case basis before making a decision (Mannheim and Wilkins 1955). If discretion is incorporated into the system and the practitioner can override the predictive scheme, such overrides may occur with a frequency closely related to the complexity and dimensions of the scheme. If such discretion is limited, shoddy data collection practices may occur to compensate for the additional burden upon the practitioner. Finally, cumbersome and overly sophisticated predictive systems will be incomprehensible to the individuals to whom they pertain. The criminal justice system is not served by an instrument that fails to clarify to the offender the criteria underlying its decisions.

One way to maximize parsimony is to limit the predictive system to those variables that add measurably to the predictive power of a scheme. The identification of these variables may pose a problem as a variable may exercise both direct and indirect effects on the criterion (predicted) variables. Multivariate causal models, such as those in path analysis, may be useful (Land 1969). Even if only direct effects are considered, the identification of the most important predictor variables may be problematic as, in analytical techniques such as multiple regression, the order in which they are entered in an equation can profoundly affect their apparent explanatory power. Thus, the stepwise technique within the general linear approaches might be employed. Generally, this technique involves a prioritization of variables at each stage of the equation-building process. That is, the first variable to enter the equation is that with the greatest initial association with the predictive criterion (e.g. recidivism). The second variable entered is that which, in combination with the first, affords the highest association. The procedure continues in a similar manner until the further addition of variables no longer yields a statistically significant increment of predictive power. At each stage, as well, variables may be deleted from the equation if, upon the addition of a new variable at that stage, the information provided by the resulting combination of variables is redundant (Klecka 1975).

The issue of variable redundancy or overlap is central to the objective of parsimony and the selection of a statistical method for prediction efforts. While the linear procedures of regression and discriminant analysis are tailor-made to eliminate redundancy, 'accounting' schemes that have been used in criminological predictions, such as the Burgess method (this will be discussed shortly), merely combine variables in an additive fashion without regard for redundancy. Thus, the extent to which they measure the same thing, and the manner in which they are interrelated, is obscured. Aside from the general linear models, a technique such as factor analysis, which reduces highly intercorrelated variables to one common factor, can be used to tackle the problem of overlap (Rummel 1970). This factor can then be entered as a variable into a simple accounting scheme, linear model, or other system and be measured accordingly.

The assumptions of a given statistical technique are also relevant. The accounting schemes and the general linear techniques usually assume linearity and additivity of these variables in relation to the criterion. Thus a straight-line relationship is assumed to exist, with the score of the criterion increasing by specified units in relation to a corresponding increase or decrease in the predictor variables. Interaction terms can be included in regression equations in recognition of the interactive effect of two variables. Other techniques also can accommodate variable interaction. In addition, in regression variable transformations can be undertaken to reflect non-linear relationships (Neter and Wasserman 1974).

Another element in the combination of variables, recommended early by the Gluecks (1950), is that of weighting. Predictor variables can be provided differential weights to reflect their relative influence on the outcome variable. Some of the earlier, and even many current, actuarial schemes have lacked such weighting. Weighting is an integral part of some methods. Multiple regression, for example, provides coefficients (correlation coefficients) reflecting the predictive yield of each independent variable in an equation when all other variables are controlled.

The level of measurement of both the predictor and outcome variables is also germane to the selection of a statistical method, as well as to the reliability of a predictive model. Generally, the more precise the level of measurement, the greater the likelihood of error in rating subjects (or other units of analysis) on the relevant variables. Clearly, it is easier to discern a subject's sex or race than his or her IQ. Similarly, the dichotomization of IQ into 'low' and 'high' will be less problematic than giving the subject a specific score. In categorical measures, only cases located near cutting-points will be misclassified. Misclassification can be avoided by eliminating such cases or scores from the analysis. An IQ score may be affected by the condition of the subject on the day of assessment, by the environment in which the test is administered, by the characteristics of those administering it, and by countless other factors. No single assessment can be completely reliable, even assuming the perfect internal validity of the instrument. Providing that measurement error is evenly distributed across a sample, the analysis will be affected as far as the relationship between this independent variable and the outcome variable is concerned (Lewis-Beck 1980). However, if an interaction exists between particular characteristics of subjects and those of the testing environment, a great deal of variation in measurement error may occur from one subject to another (Campbell and Stanley 1963).

The implications of measurement error become most apparent during the development of a predictive model. The correct procedure in such efforts involves the selection of a *construction* sample and the use of an existing data base to formulate the preliminary model. This model is then tested against a comparable *validation* sample to determine the extent to which its predictive power is maintained for other samples.

The use of a second sample to test a predictive model is important for several reasons (Frances H. Simon 1971). First, some of the associations between the postulated predictor variables and the criterion or dependent variable in the construction sample may be spurious or inflated by chance. This is so because no two samples are identical and the greater the number of variables one uses, the greater the possibility that one or two of them stand out in a way that will not occur in another sample drawn. One may, for example, have drawn a sample of offenders comprising an atypical proportion of narcotics or multiple drug users, as it is difficult to draw a sample that is representative of a designated population in every respect. In such a sample, drug use may be strongly associated with recidivism, whereas, in subsequent samples drawn, the association might be considerably weaker simply because of the lower prevalence of drug users. Many other characteristics of a sample or events to which the sample is exposed may be unique, as one cannot possibly match samples on every possible predictive dimension.

Thus one has to see whether the predictive associations apply to other cases or the extent to which they are bound to the sample.

To understand more fully the need for validation, it might be helpful to draw an analogy from the food industry. Let us suppose that a company producing cereal was interested in developing a new product and had some general idea as to the direction it wanted to take. Upon completing a preliminary product, the company consults with its food-tasters and is advised that some refinement is necessary. After further refinement, more testing is done, and this process of refinement and feedback continues for some time. Finally, a point is reached (according to some specified criteria) where there is enough consensus among the food-tasters to test the product on the market. Will another sample of food-tasters (even if drawn from the same population as the original tasters) arrive at the same conclusions? It is likely that the product is more suited to the first group because they were involved in the development of the product – this could therefore be a biased sample. One, therefore, has to see the extent to which a second sample of tasters, not involved in the product's development, agrees with the first. The loss of support for the product or a predictive model, from one sample to another, is referred to as *shrinkage*. One of the best ways to minimize shrinkage is to maximize the size of the construction sample. In that way, this original sample is less likely to be atypical of the general population from which other samples may be drawn.

A related reason for validating a prediction model concerns the base rate problem. The proportion of the construction sample engaged in the predicted behaviour (e.g. violent crime) must be similar to the rate of violence in the population to which the predictions are being applied. If the construction sample is selected retrospectively so as to include an equal number of violent and non-violent individuals, the predictions drawn from these comparisons cannot be applied, without the necessary statistical adjustments, to a population of offenders containing merely a small proportion of violent people. If these adjustments are not made, a considerable number of false positives or overpredictions of violence may result.

A third reason for validating a prediction model is that the relative importance of predictors, as well as the nature of their interactions, may change over time. Changing social influences on criminality or criminal justice policies may alter offenders' behaviour patterns. The way to gauge these changes is to validate a predictive instrument periodically.

The validation of a predictive model can also be impeded by measurement errors in a study. The greater the measurement error, the greater the shrinkage in subsequent samples will be as the errors become further compounded with each successive sample to which the predictive system is applied. That is because the system itself, if it is periodically updated, will now be based on a number of samples in which shrinkage (due partly to measurement error) occurred. It may be argued, from a purely mathematical point of view, that the increasing size of the data base will lend greater credence to the predictive model as the errors of measurement offset one another. This is true, however, only if such errors are 'random.' If measurement criteria or scores change over time or location as the data base is expanded, this will not be the case. Systematic changes in police, judicial, and correctional record-keeping do occur over time and across jurisdictions. These changes will have less of an effect on categorical than on interval level data, minimizing shrinkage for models comprising the more crudely measured variables.

One of the areas in which measurement error has been most pronounced concerns the outcome or criterion variable in prediction, such as that of offender recidivism. Criminal justice agencies are likely to underestimate relapses in criminality simply because they cannot identify and apprehend the perpetrators of many offences. There are also difficulties in the way recidivism is measured. It can be argued that recidivism is a continuous rather than dichotomous variable and that a person's rate of recidivism must be calculated in relation to the time he or she is at risk to recidivate (Harris and Moitra 1978).

On another level, parametric statistics that deal primarily with continuous variables contain assumptions that, if violated, may provide 'biased' estimates of an outcome variable. Assumptions in regression analysis such as the normal distribution and equal variances of a dependent variable over the various observations of an independent variable(s) must obtain or serious estimation problems may result. Non-parametric methods, however, because they lack such assumptions, are more robust in that the shrinkage of a predictive model from one sample to another is likely to be less pronounced. By using less refined data and analytical methods, however, one is sacrificing precision, which, in the realm of prediction, means the ability to make precise (not to be confused with accurate) predictions of behaviour. Thus the use of parametric statistics with interval-level variables can yield predictions as to the degree of seriousness of an offender's future conduct, whereas categorical data and non-parametric analysis can provide only the likelihood of various outcome scenarios for more crude dimensions of behaviour (e.g. violent versus non-violent behaviour).

A further point that needs to be addressed in the selection of a statistical technique is that of population homogeneity. Can one assume, for example, that a single predictive model will be equally powerful for different population subgroups? If, for example, alcohol abuse is entered into a model because it is found that it is a good predictor of recidivism, can it be safely assumed that such abuse is equally dangerous among women as among men, or among the old as among the young, for those of higher as opposed to lower social status, for those with no assaultive history as for those with such a history? By not taking into consideration what is, in a sense, an interaction between a given predictor item and certain individual characteristics, the predictive power of the model is weakened because it may be applied to segments of the population to which it is largely irrelevant. One way to circumvent this problem is to classify the concerned population initially into the most homogeneous groups (through techniques such as association analysis) and then to develop separate predictive models for each group.

One important caution, relating to the predictive power of a model, concerns the base rate problem. Predicting violence is said to be difficult because of the generally low prevalence of such behaviour. All other things being equal, predicting an event that occurs infrequently is more difficult than predicting one that occurs more often. In the case of our table, the task of prediction would even be more difficult, and predictive power poorer, if the overall likelihood of success, following release from prison, were lower.

The overall success rate of the hypothetical sample of offenders in the table is about 42 per cent. Suppose only 10 per cent of these offenders failed to recidivate following their release. This number is so small that the differences in success rates among the categories (those with no prior offences, those with one prior offence, etc) could not be as pronounced as with a larger overall success rate. Probably the best prediction when the overall success rate is 10 per cent is simply to predict that all persons will recidivate. This prediction will be correct in nine out of ten cases. When the base rates of success or failure are extremely high or low, predicting that all will experience the same fate as the modal category is often the best approach. It is when the base rates are moderate (e.g. from 30 per cent to 70 per cent) that prediction models are most useful (Frances H. Simon 1971).

Following is a brief discussion of statistical methods that have been used, evaluated, or proposed for predictive efforts. No attempt is made to be exhaustive; in fact, only a representative technique (the best known) in each class is presented.

Burgess method

Included here are a class of simple actuarial tables that assume linear, additive relationships among the predictor and criterion variables used. The first such table was developed in 1928 by Ernest Burgess on the basis of a population of Illinois parolees (Mannheim and Wilkins 1965). Burgess examined 21 factors related to the possibility of successful parole outcome. Each factor was arbitrarily given a maximum value of one point. If an individual belonged to a category on a particular factor that had a parole violation rate under that of the whole population, he or she received a favourable point. The person's total score over the 21 factors was then tallied to determine his or her general class in terms of the probability of recidivism. The major modification of this technique was devised by the Gluecks (1950), who correlated each predictive factor with the outcome variable to determine its relevance in distinguishing between parole success and failure. These factors were then weighted according to the extent of this correlation.

One advantage of these relatively crude prediction tables is the simplicity with which they can be used by practitioners. Also, the categorical data that they contain are less subject to measurement error and are distribution-free. Thus this technique can be quite robust, minimizing shrinkage from one sample to another. The major deficiency of these tables is that they do not provide for variable overlap or interaction. Variable overlap creates redundancy (some highly intercorrelated variables may virtually measure the same thing), and the lack of recognition of variable interactions undermines the predictive power of such tables.

Configural analysis

Configural analysis is a class of techniques in which an initially undifferentiated population is subdivided into groups according to some criterion. This criterion can be the maximization of the groups' homogeneity, in which case the objective is a taxonomic one – probably the best-known technique here is association analysis (Williams and Lambert 1959). Predictions can then be made on the basis of these classifications; however, the classifications produced by association analysis do no provide the best discrimination among groups in terms of their future behaviour because the formation of the groups is based on a homogeneity rather than outcome criterion (e.g. recidivism).

The most appropriate configural method in the development of groups that are distinguished on the basis of an outcome criterion is predictive attribute analysis (Wilkins and MacNaughton-Smith 1964). This method involves the initial subdivision of a sample into two groups on the basis of that factor (usually dichotomous) most strongly associated with the predictive criterion. Thus, if recidivism is the criterion and sex is the variable most closely related to it for a sample, offenders would first be divided according to sex. The resulting two groups are then further subdivided into two groups apiece based on the best predictor in each group. These factors can, of course, be different for the two groups as, for example, the predictive variables for men and women may differ considerably. This process of sub-division continues until no factors significantly related to the outcome criterion remain. The procedure thus provides a hierarchical method of of-fender classification, whereby groups can be situated on a continuum according to their probability of success on a criterion.

Configural analysis takes into account variable interactions through the process of group division. It also accommodates the heterogeneity of of-fender populations by providing varying predictions for different sub-populations rather than applying the same predictive model to the entire population. The categorical data used make it attractive to practitioners.

A major disadvantage of configural analysis is the need to reclassify en-tire populations if variable cut-off points are altered by social or policy changes (Babst, Gottfredson, and Ballard 1968). Let us suppose that the variable 'drug use' was formerly dichotomized into the categories of 'infre-quent' and 'frequent,' with the cutting-point being usage twice a week. An increasing frequency of use in the general population may warrant the in-crease of the cutting-point to three times per week to differentiate casual from intensive use. The resulting reclassification may require reshuffling the membership of virtually every group formed. The same consequence would occur with the finding that, as cases are added to the data base, the factors on the basis of which the original groups were formed were changing in their respective relevance to the outcome criterion. Configural analysis also does not indicate the degree of intercorrelation or the relative impor-tance of the predictor variables within any subpopulation (Brown 1978).

Multiple regression

In multiple regression, equations are developed to describe the relationship between a number of independent variables and the outcome (dependent) variable. This relationship is usually assumed to be linear and additive with a dependent variable varying in relation to the combined variation of the in-dependent variables. Each variable possesses a weight (regression coeffi-cient) that describes the direct effect of that variable on the dependent variable, controlling for the remaining variables in the equation. Thus it is possible to ascertain the relative importance of each variable in the system. However, because the magnitude of these coefficients differs according to the order in which they were entered into the model, the stepwise procedure elaborated above can be recommended in most instances. Because each coefficient represents a direct effect on the outcome variable, with all other variables in the system controlled, the problems of variable intercorrelation and overlap are largely avoided.

As multiple regression is primarily used in the analysis of interval-level data, it can provide precise predictions related to such outcome criteria as the likelihood and seriousness of future criminal violations. At the same time, such precision renders the technique more vulnerable to measurement error and the violation of assumptions regarding error terms (Palmer and Carlson 1978). Thus shrinkage from sample to sample tends to be greater for such methods than for those involving categorical data. Like all techniques other than the configural approach, multiple regression models are usually based on entire populations and thus assume population homogeneity. This assumption can be avoided, however, by combining the two techniques. Thus, a population can be classified into groups as homogeneous as is possible through association analysis or a related technique and separate regression equations can be developed for each subpopulation thereby obtained. This dual approach has been said to yield better results than the use of either technique alone (Sampson 1974). Generally speaking, regression does not address the issue of independent variable interaction, although interaction terms can be included in an equation.

Multidiscriminant analysis

Somewhat similar to regression analysis with a dichotomous dependent variable is multidiscriminant analysis (Gottfredson and Gottfredson 1979). This technique reverses the procedure of most multivariate methods by dealing with a priori groups in developing a linear additive model that best discriminates between the existing groups. Thus selected variables are provided weights on the basis of their ability to discriminate between the groups (on some criterion such as parole outcome and a statistical criterion such as the F-ratio). The variables ultimately incorporated into the model will be those that, in combination, best differentiate the groups. Here again, a stepwise procedure is frequently employed to develop the most parsimonious model. Thus one can take two groups of parolees, one of which has had a successful outcome and the other which has not. Then an equation is developed comprising those variables (and their coefficients) that provide maximum discrimination between parole success and failure for the sample. This equation can then be used as a classificatory device to place subsequent individuals in one group or the other based on their scores on each variable and the relative weight of these variables. The entire system can then be tested against a person's actual performance.

The assumptions of discriminant analysis are less restrictive than those for regression analysis with a categorical dependent variable. These include the normal distribution of the discriminating variables within each group, a statistically significant difference in the group means on each variable, similar group variances of the variables, and the additive rather than the interactive relationships among the discriminating variables.

Log-linear analysis

This technique has only recently been proposed for use in criminological prediction (Solomon 1976). Log-linear analysis provides a means by which linear models can be developed for categorical variables, including the interaction effects of independent variables. This technique examines all conceivable ways in which each independent variable can affect the dependent variable (both directly and interactively with the other independent variables). Even if all the variables are dichotomous, this will produce a cell count of 2^x, the exponent x representing the number of independent variables. Through a stepwise procedure, only those main and interactive effects that significantly contribute to the development of a parsimonious model are retained. This is done through initially determining the extent of associations between all categories of the hypothesized predictive variables and the outcome variable through chi-square tests of independence. Presuming there is a significant association, variables are then introduced, through the stepwise approach, based on the criterion that they significantly reduce the chi-square value of the overall model. This thereby provides the model that best explains (the best fit) the observed cell frequencies. It should be stressed that the higher the chi-square value, the greater the departure of the observed from the expected (according to the null hypothesis of independence between the relevant variables) frequencies. Through the conversion of cell counts to logarithms, an additive model is obtained as in regression. This model will, as mentioned, comprise coefficients pertaining to those main and interactive effects that are retained after all effects from the saturated model (all conceivable effects of the independent variables on the dependent variable) that detract from parsimony are omitted (van Alstyne and Gottfredson 1978). Probabilities relating to the predictive criterion (e.g. parole success) can be calculated on the basis of the final model.

Log-linear analysis is attractive because of its sophisticated handling of categorical data, its consideration of predictor variable interactions, its weighting of both main and interactive effects, and its ability to identify the most parsimonious subset of predictors among a group of variables. Its one major drawback is its requirement of a large number of cases for even relatively few variables due to the number of cells necessary to accommodate all the categories of the independent variables and their interactions.

Other techniques

All the methods enumerated above are capable of providing the practitioner with statments relating to the probability of alternative outcomes, although some techniques provide these in a more direct fashion than others. Multiple regression, for example, can provide precise predictions of future behaviour and can also serve as a taxonomic device by providing a continuous distribution of offenders according to the risk they pose to society. One can additionally compute the probabilities of various outcomes (e.g. recidivism) for the offender categories thereby formed. For the techniques using categorical outcome criteria, probabilities are readily computed from the existing data base.

Some of the most sophisticated probability models include such techniques as network analysis, in which the probability of various event sequences is computed based on a knowledge of these events, as well as their interrelationships (Standards Evaluation and Statistical Analysis Section 1981). This might include the delineation of various situational scenarios that a designated type of person might experience. Thus the characteristics of an individual and situations he or she is likely to encounter (as well as their likelihood) are taken into account, as are the expected reactions to these. This type of scheme is testable by computer simulations, particularly (although not exclusively) if a deterministic system is assumed. The anticipation of complex scenarios is a problematic task, as the passage of time inevitably nullifies and necessitates modification of the scheme. This is due to the fact that change in merely one link in the network will alter all the projected scenarios. A more modest approach would be to assume a Markhov process whereby behaviour at one point in the sequence is assumed to be dependent only on the individual's state (condition) at the previous point, rather than on a multitude of prior decision points (Greenberg 1979).

Several comparisons have been undertaken to determine which statistical method is superior in terms of such criteria as predictive power, assumptions of the technique, and shrinkage from construction to validation samples. These comparisons have involved the application of the different techniques to the same sample of offenders and data set. They have primarily pertained to the Burgess method, configural analysis, multiple regression, and log-linear analysis. These studies overwhelmingly indicate that there is little to choose in terms of explanatory power between these techniques and that the slight advantage, in this regard, of the more sophisticated multivariate techniques tends to be offset by the greater shrinkage encountered due to measurement error (Frances H. Simon 1971). The implication of these findings is that the selection of a method be based on other than statistical criteria – e.g. the nature of the data base and the method most usable by decision-makers in the criminal justice system. Another implication is that mathematical wizardry will not resolve the problems of prediction. These problems can be tackled only through improved offender classification procedures, the use of more valid and reliable data bases, and more careful variable selection, if they can be resolved at all.

Conclusion

The expansion of the role of prediction in criminal justice decision-making is under way. One widely accepted approach, at various levels of the criminal justice system, is the use of predictive guidelines. Such guidelines are based on the assumption of the superiority of statistical over clinical methods in prediction and are oriented towards the dual concerns of applying equitable criteria across cases while retaining sufficient discretion for decision-makers to consider the idiosyncratic aspects of a case.

There is a growing recognition of the fact that prediction, at least at the informal level, already underlies the actions of personnel within the criminal justice system, as it does all social behaviour. This being the case, it can be argued that the arbitrary and subjective nature of current predictions should be replaced by a more structured approach. There is also support for the belief that the prediction of offender behaviour should play a primary role in sentencing, so that we can become more selective in the use of prisons in order to incapacitate a larger proportion of dangerous offenders. Moreover, the systematic application of empirically based predictions can enhance the parsimonious use of criminal justice resources, such as prison space, during the current era of fiscal restraint.

Predictive guidelines, precisely because of their scientific basis and, hence, legitimacy, must be regarded with extreme prudence because of their inherent dangers and limitations. Excessive reliance on prediction in sentencing will result in an undermining of the retribution/desert principles of justice and, hence, can potentially lead to a loss of public confidence in the criminal justice system. The public's perception that the criminal justice system does not endeavour to address the grievances of crime victims can lead to vigilantism. An over-reliance on prediction may place a disproportionate number of minority persons in high-risk groups, thereby increasing the concentration of these people in our institutions – a situation that may exacerbate inter-racial conflicts (Gabor 1985). These consequences can off-set any possible crime-preventive gains achieved through improved prediction.

If made explicit, predictions may also foster self-fulfilling prophecies by placing people in roles that are difficult to discard. These roles reinforce, rather than rectify, social inequities. Further, inherent in any statistical prediction scheme is error, and experience thus far with prediction suggests that the most tolerated form of error is the false positive – the mistaken belief that an individual poses some form of threat to society. Individual civil liberties can be jeopardized by predictive guidelines predicated on the calculation of the costs and benefits of various sentencing policies to society as a whole.

The evidence presented points to serious limitations in our ability to predict criminal behaviour. No variable or factor has escaped controversy in relation to its predictive value, and very few have been spared serious criticism on ethical grounds.

Nevertheless, some variables are more robust in their explanatory power than others. As a general observation, the ascribed variables of sex, race/ethnicity, and age appear to be better predictors of conduct than are attributes over which people exercise somewhat greater control – personality, social status, and the like. This may partly result from the greater consistency and, hence, predictability of societal responses towards persons of differing status on these ascribed variables. Thus, observed differences in the criminal behaviour of the two sexes, of different racial or ethnic groups, and of persons of varying age groups can at least partly be attributed to their differential treatment by the criminal justice system. The observed differences that remain, once this bias is discounted, may be largely due to differential treatment by society at large. The extent to which differential behaviour exists beyond that attributable to criminal justice system bias or societal response – that is to say, due to biological factors – is, not surprisingly, a subject involving little consensus.

The evidence suggests that less cross-cultural variation exists in the relative participation in crime of the two sexes and of varying age groups than is the case for different racial or ethnic groups. This could again be due to a greater consistency, on the global level, in the treatment of women and the young, than in the treatment of any racial or ethnic group. The evidence does suggest, however, that historical changes within societies are more apt to occasion changes in the criminal behaviour of racial or ethnic groups than they are to narrow the gap between the sexes or varying age groups.

The feminist movement in the West, for example, has not drastically altered the proportional participation of females in most types of traditional crime. In fact, the gap between the sexes has widened, over the past two decades, for some violent offences.

Predicting that a group is more susceptible to criminal behaviour does not mean that it is more likely to be highly active, to engage in more serious criminal acts, or to have higher recidivism rates than some other group. Little is known about the criminal careers of female offenders. The information that does exist in relation to the selectively few women processed by the criminal justice system is hardly comparable to that dealing with men. In the realm of race, American studies documenting the greater prevalence of crime in the black community disagree as to the extent to which black and white offenders differ in the rate and seriousness of their criminal activity. It has fairly consistently been observed, however, that young offenders are more highly active and are greater recidivism risks than are their elders. Studies of the relationship between age and crime are, however, fraught with methodological flaws.

Problems in method may be partly responsible for the apparently greater predictive utility of ascribed over what have been called acquired variables. Problems in measurement abound in the identification of personality traits, social status, criminal history, and substance abuse. The lack of high correlations between some of these variables and various indicators of criminality may be due, to some extent at least, to the difficulty in developing valid and reliable measures of these variables. The measurement of sex, age, and, to a lesser degree, race is more facile, as is that of some biological variables, such as pulse rate and skin conductance. Nevertheless, variables such as criminal history and substance abuse have been quite robust in predicting recidivism and, often, the rate of criminality.

A major paradox is that ascribed variables, which are the best predictors of criminal behaviour (at least in terms of susceptibility to criminality), are least likely to be employed in criminal justice policy. Constitutional and statutory safeguards in many countries preclude the differential treatment of persons on the basis of sex, race, ethnicity, and, increasingly, age. Further, punitive intervention (including coerced therapy) by the criminal justice system into the lives of people merely susceptible, and not yet demonstrating a proclivity, towards criminal behaviour would face opposition because of the violation of the principle of the presumption of innocence. The documentation of the importance of these variables in predicting criminality can nevertheless be valuable in the development of remedial social programs.

Aside from measurement error, several factors will continue to compromise predictive efforts. First, the criminal justice system data on which most criminological predictions are based do not accurately reflect offender behaviour, as the system reactions culminating in official processing are themselves unpredictable. The use of alternative data sources, such as self-reported criminal behaviour, will also continue to be questioned because of their reliance on the truthfulness of respondents and the multitude of different measurement instruments used.

A second problem stems from the subjective or symbolic nature of some variables. In order to determine the full impact of variables such as race and social class, one must surmount more than the obstacles involved in their objective measurement. A person's identification with a given group will undoubtedly affect his or her reaction to the status of that group. His lineage may indicate that he is primarily Caucasian, but if he is reared in a black neighbourhood, he is likely to identify with that race. Similarly, if one has a low income, one may perceive this state as a temporary condition or as one from which one cannot extricate oneself. These identifications and perceptions can profoundly influence behaviour and are, in turn, affected by many personality, familial, and social factors.

A third major factor undermining prediction is the situational element in all human behaviour – the effects on behaviour of such things as the physical environment, provocations, and the presence of drugs, alcohol, and weapons. Studies dealing with this element have merely attempted to determine the independent effects of situational factors on behaviour. Because an individual's personality will affect his or her choice of situations, as well as his or her reactions to these, situational and personality variables must be viewed in concert. Thus, the likely outcomes of the exposure of varying persons to varying situations must be determined. More difficult, still, is the anticipation of the situations a person will actually encounter.

The effect of the environment and specific situations on behaviour may vary from one offender to the next. While hard-core or pathological offenders might commit crimes regardless of the conditions in which they live, most offenders are probably responsive to changes in their circumstances. As Walker (1980) has said, there are opportunity-makers and opportunity-takers. The more offenders there are in the latter category, the more relevant is the situational factor in criminological prediction.

Aside from the difficulties involved in anticipating the situations a person will come across, problems arise in measuring the impact of situations. It is difficult to isolate the effect of the situation from the effects of personality and prior experience on behaviour. Also, situations are harder to categorize than are such static variables as race, sex, and criminal history. They are varied in their intensity and duration. They may present varying levels of threat or provocation. They may engender differing levels of fear or hostility depending on one's personal experiences and perceptions of the often subtle or ambiguous cues emitted in many situations.

We have also shown that the mathematical techniques used to combine information are not always relevant to the predictive ability of a given set of variables. This is because all these techniques are limited in some respects. The assumptions of existing predictive methods are based on gross over-simplifications of the world in which offenders actually live. These techniques have assumed such things as the independence of predictor variables, linearity in their relationships with criterion variables, and recursive (non-reciprocal) causal relationships among the variables in a given causal model. Moreover, the number of variables generally used in prediction efforts have been few and have most often lacked the interdisciplinary nature required for serious efforts.

It is important to qualify these pessimistic remarks by stating that the nature of the dependent or criterion variable is also instrumental in determining the outcome of predictions. The more specific the predictions we are trying to make – in terms of the nature, timing, or location of an offence – the less likely we are to succeed. Human behaviour often lacks regularity or consistency. 'Out-of-character' episodes and the innumerable situations to which people are exposed affect the specific dimensions of behaviour. Most people commit at least some technical violations of the law. However, it may be reasonable to believe that greater consistency exists on critical, fundamental dimensions such as the general pursuit of a law-abiding as opposed to anti-social life-style. In this regard, predictions of recidivism have been far more reliable than predictions of its specific dimensions.

One final point. Our ability to predict is contingent on the prevalence of what we are predicting. Correct predictions of violent recidivism (true positives) will be made more frequently in areas where the base rates of violent recidivism are higher. The more unlikely an event, the less likely we are to predict its occurrence, all other things being equal.

Thus, while the potential of the prediction enterprise should not be exaggerated, the use of predictive information furnished by scientific inquiry cannot be ignored in criminal justice system decisions. While limitations do exist in the official data upon which predictive statements are most often based, to suggest that such data are totally flawed and devoid of any intrinsic meaning would be to suggest that the entire system is a sham, reacting only capriciously to perceived unlawful behaviour. To suggest that no variable is objectively useful as a predictor of behaviour would be to suggest that all human behaviour is capricious and totally free of external constraints. Finally, to suggest that the situational element in behaviour is all important would be to suggest that human beings are identical and devoid of any essence.

It is also important to bear in mind that while predicting criminal behaviour may be plagued by many inherent limitations and ethical objections, neglecting it is ignoring the reality of human decision-making. Also, precluding predictions in criminal justice decisions elevates, to a preeminent status, our concern with past behaviour and our assessments about the offender's culpability for it. Thus human decision-makers, rather than making scientific (albeit unreliable) statements about future risks, will merely resort to passing superhuman judgments about the immorality of behaviour that has already taken place.

Bibliography

Adams, Susan G. 1978 *The Female Offender: A Statistical Perspective* Ottawa: Ministry of the Solicitor General

Adler, Freda 1975 *Sisters in Crime* New York: McGraw-Hill

Alexander, Franz and William Healy 1935 *Roots of Crime* New York: Knopf

American Correctional Association 1975 *Correctional Classification and Treatment* Cincinnati, Ohio: W.H. Anderson

American Friends Service Committee 1972 *Struggle for Justice: A Report on Crime and Punishment in America* New York: Hill and Wang

Amir, Menachem 1971 *Patterns in Forcible Rape* Chicago: University of Chicago Press

Ares, Charles E., Anne Rankin and Herbert Sturz 1963 'The Manhattan Bail Project: An Interim Report on the Use of Pre-trial Parole' *New York University Law Review* 38:71–92

Ascher, William 1978 *Forecasting: An Appraisal for Policy-Makers and Planners* Baltimore, Md: The John Hopkins University Press

Ash, P. 1949 'The Reliability of Psychiatric Diagnosis' *The Journal of Abnormal and Social Psychology* 44:272–6

Babst, Dean V., Don M. Gottfredson and Kelley B. Ballard 1968 'Comparison of Multiple Regression and Configural Analysis Techniques for Developing Base Expectancy Tables' *Journal of Research in Crime and Delinquency* 5(1):72–80

Babst, Dean V., Mary Koval and M.G. Neithercutt 1972 'Relationship of Time Served to Parole Outcome for Different Classifications of Burglars Based on Males Paroled in Fifty Jurisdictions in 1968 and 1969' *Journal of Research in Crime and Delinquency* 9(2):99–116

Baird, Christopher, Richard Heinz and Brian J. Bemus 1979 *The Wisconsin Case Classification/Staff Development Project: A Two Year Follow-up Report* Wisconsin Division of Corrections, July

Ball, John C., Lawrence Rosen, John A. Flueck and David Nurco 1981 'The Criminality of Heroin Addicts When Addicted and When Off Opiates' in James A. Inciardi *The Drugs-Crime Connection* Beverly Hills, Cal: Sage Publications

Bartollas, Clemens and Stuart J. Miller 1978 *Correctional Administration: Theory and Practice* New York: McGraw-Hill

Beck, James L. and Peter B. Hoffman 1976 'Time Served and Release Performance: A Research Note' *Journal of Research in Crime and Delinquency* 13(2):127-32

Bem, D. and D. Funder 1978 'Predicting More of the People More of the Time: Assessing the Personality of Situations' *Psychological Review* 85:485-501

Berelson, Bernard and Gary A. Steiner 1964 *Human Behavior: An Inventory of Scientific Findings* New York: Harcourt, Brace and World

Blum, Richard H. 1969 *Society and Drugs* San Francisco: Jossey-Blass

Blumstein, Alfred and Jacqueline Cohen 1979 'Estimation of Individual Crime Rates from Arrest Records' *Journal of Criminal Law and Criminology* 70(4)

Blumstein, Alfred and Elizabeth Graddy 1982 'Prevalence and Recidivism in Index Arrests: A Feedback Model' *Law and Society Review* 16(2):265-90

Boggs, Sarah L. 'Urban Crime Patterns' 1965 *American Sociological Review* 30:899-908

Bohnstedt, Marvin 1979 'Variables Common to Pre-trial Sentencing/Parole Release and Institutional Custody Classification Instruments' paper presented at the Annual Meeting of the American Society of Criminology, Philadelphia, November

Boland, Barbara and James Q. Wilson 1978 'Age, Crime and Punishment' *The Public Interest* 51

Bonger, Willem 1916 *Criminality and Economic Conditions* Boston: Little Brown

Bottomley, A. Keith 1973 'Parole Decisions in a Long-Term Closed Prison' *British Journal of Criminology* 13(1):26-40

Bottoms, Anthony E. 1977 'Reflections on the Renaissance of Dangerousness' *Howard Journal of Penology and Crime Prevention* 16(2):70-6

Brantingham, Paul J. and Frederic Faust 1976 'A Conceptual Model of Crime Prevention' *Crime and Delinquency* 22:284-96

Brooks, D.N. 1974 'Recognition, Memory and Head Injury' *Journal of Neurology, Neurosurgery and Psychiatry* 37(7):794-801

Brown, Lawrence D. 1978 'The Development of a Parole Classification System Using Discriminant Analysis' *Journal of Research in Crime and Delinquency* 15(1):92-108

Bullock, Henry A. 1955 'Urban Homicide in Theory and Fact' *Journal of Criminal Law, Criminology and Police Science* 45(1):565-75

Calvin, Allen D. 1981 'Unemployment among Black Youths, Demographics and Crime' *Crime and Delinquency* 27(2):234-44

Campbell, Donald T. and Julian C. Stanley 1963 *Experimental and Quasi-Experimental Designs for Research* Chicago: Rand McNally

Canadian Committee on Corrections Report 1969 *Toward Unity: Criminal Justice and Corrections* Ottawa: Queen's Printer

Carter, Donald L. and Kim Q. Hill 1973 'The Criminal's Image of the City and Urban Crime Patterns' *Social Science Quarterly* 57(3):597-607

Chelimsky, E. and E. Dahmann 1981 *Career Criminal Program National Evaluation: Final Report* Washington, D.C.: U.S. Department of Justice

Clarke, Ronald V.G. 1983 'Situational Crime Prevention: Its Theoretical Basis and Practical Scope' in Michael Tonry and Norval Morris eds *Crime and Justice: An Annual Review of Research* Chicago: University of Chicago Press, 225-56

Clarke, Ronald V.G. and Patricia Mayhew 1980 *Designing out Crime* London: Her Majesty's Stationery Office

Clear, Todd R., John D. Hewitt and Robert M. Rigoli 1978 'Discretion and the Determinate Sentence: Its Distribution, Control and Effect on Time Served' *Crime and Delinquency* 24(4):428-45

Clemmer, Donald 1940 *The Prison Community* New York: Rinehart and Co

Cloward, Richard and Lloyd D. Ohlin 1960 *Delinquency and Opportunity* New York: The Free Press

Cockett, R. 1973 'Habituation to Criminal Behaviour' *British Journal of Criminology* 13(4):384-9

Cocozza, Joseph J., Mary E. Melick and Henry J. Steadman 1978 'Trends in Violent Crime among Ex-Mental Patients' *Criminology* 16(3):317-34

Cohen, Albert K. 1955 *Delinquent Boys* New York: The Free Press

Cohen, Albert K., George F. Cole and Robert G. Bailey eds 1976 *Prison Violence* Lexington, Mass: D.C. Heath

Cohen, Lawrence E. and David Cantor 1981 'Residential Burglary in the United States: Lifestyle and Demographic Factors Associated with the Probability of Victimization' *Journal of Research in Crime and Delinquency* 18(1):113-27

Commission of Inquiry into the Non-Medical Use of Drugs 1973 *Final Report* Ottawa: Information Canada

Conklin, John E. 1981 *Criminology* New York: Macmillan

Conner, Walter 1972 *Deviance in Soviet Society: Crime, Delinquency, Alcoholism* New York: Columbia University Press

Cormier, B.M., M. Kennedy, J.M. Sangowicz, and M. Trottier 1961 'Criminal Acting out in Cases of Reactive Depression' *Canadian Journal of Corrections* 3(1):38-50

Cormier, Bruno M. 1965 'The Family and Delinquency' *Sciences de l'homme: Contributions à l'étude* 6:83–117

Cormier, Bruno M., J.M. Sangowicz, Miriam Kennedy and Anthony T. Galardo 1964 'Episodic Recidivism' *Proceedings of the Fourth Research Conference in Delinquency and Criminology* Montreal: Quebec Society of Criminology, 171–93

Crites, Laura 1976 *The Female Offender* Lexington, Mass: D.C. Heath

Curtis, Lynn A. 1976 *Criminal Violence* Lexington, Mass: D.C. Heath

Davies, James C. 1962 'Toward a Theory of Revolution' *American Sociological Review* 27:5–19

Dershowitz, Alan 1974 'The Origins of Preventive Confinement in Anglo-American Law. Part I: The English Experience' *University of Cincinnati Law Review* 43:1–60

Dinitz, Simon 1981 'Preventing Juvenile Crime and Delinquency' lecture at the 25th Congress of the International Union of Local Authorities, Columbus, Ohio, 23 June

Dugdale, Richard L. 1877 *The Jukes* New York: Putnam

Dunn, Christopher 1980 'Prediction Problems and Decision Logic in Longitudinal Studies of Delinquency' paper presented at the Annual Meeting of the American Society of Criminology, San Francisco, 5–8 November

Efran, Michael G. 1974 'The Effect of Physical Appearance on the Judgement of Guilt, Interpersonal Attraction and Severity of Recommended Punishment in a Simulated Jury Task' *Journal of Research in Personality* 8:45–54

Elkins, Stanley 1967 'Slavery and Personality' in Richard Lazarus and Edward Opton eds *Personality* London: Cox and Wyman, 394–420

Ellinwood, E.H. 1971 'Assault and Homicide Associated with Amphetamine Abuse' *American Journal of Psychiatry* 127(9):90–5

Endler, N.S. and D. Magnusson 1976 'Toward an Interactional Psychology of Personality' *Psychological Bulletin* 83:974

Engstad, Peter A. 1975 'Environmental Opportunities and the Ecology of Crime' in Robert A. Silverman and James J. Teevan eds *Crime in Canadian Society* Toronto: Butterworths

Eysenck, Hans J. 1964 *Crime and Personality* London: Routledge and Kegan Paul

Farrington, David P. 1983 *Further Analyses of a Longitudinal Survey of Crime and Delinquency* Washington, DC: National Institute of Justice

Fattah, Ezzat A. 1977 'Deterrence: A Review of the Literature' *Canadian Journal of Criminology and Corrections* 19(2):1–119

Festinger, Leon 1957 *A Theory of Cognitive Dissonance* Stanford, Cal: Stanford University Press

Floud, Jean and Warren Young 1981 *Dangerousness and Criminal Justice* London: Heinemann

Fogel, David 1974 *We Are the Living Proof ... : The Justice Model for Corrections* 2nd edition, Cincinnati, Ohio: Anderson

Frankel, Marvin E. 1972 *Criminal Sentences* New York: Hill and Wang

Frazier, Charles E., E. Wilbur Bock and John C. Henretta 1980 'Pretrial Release and Bail Decisions: The Effects of Legal, Community and Personal Variables' *Criminology*, 18(2):162–81

Freedman, Johnathan L. 1975 *Crowding and Behavior* San Francisco: W.H. Freeman

Gabor, Thomas 1978 'Crime Displacement: The Literature and Strategies for Its Investigation' *Crime et/and Justice* 6(2):100–7

– 1981 'The Crime Displacement Phenomenon: An Empirical Examination' *Crime and Delinquency* 27(3):390–404

– 1983 'The Dangerous Criminal and Incapacitation Policies' Columbus, Ohio: PhD dissertation

– 1985 'Incapacitation Policies: Their Applicability to the Canadian Situation' *Canadian Journal of Criminology* 27(4):409–28

Gabor, Thomas and Tonia Barker 1985 'Probing the Public's Dishonesty: A Canadian Field Experiment' Ottawa: Centre of Criminology, University of Ottawa

Gabor, Thomas and Ellen Gottheil 1984 'Offender Characteristics and Spatial Mobility: An Empirical Study and Some Policy Implications' *Canadian Journal of Criminology* 26(3):267-81

Gabor, Thomas and John McFarlane 1982 'The Relationship between Urban Crowding and Crime: A Canadian Study' Ottawa: University of Ottawa

Gabor, Thomas Jody Strean, Gurnam Singh, and David Varis 1986 'Public Deviance: An Experimental Study' *Canadian Journal of Criminology* 28(1):17-29

Gendreau, Paul, Patrick G. Madden and Mary Leipciger 1980 'Predicting Recidivism with Social History Information and a Comparison of Their Predictive Power with Psychometric Variables' *Canadian Journal of Criminology* 22(3):328-36

Glaser, Daniel 1964 *The Effectiveness of a Prison and Parole System* New York: Bobbs-Merrill

Glueck, Sheldon and Eleanor Glueck 1937 *Later Criminal Careers* New York: The Commonwealth Fund

– 1940 *Juvenile Delinquents Grown up* New York: The Commonwealth Fund

– 1950 *Unraveling Juvenile Delinquency* New York: The Commonwealth Fund

Goffman, Erving 1961 *Asylums: Essays on the Social Situation of Mental*

Patients and Other Inmates Garden City, NY: Doubleday

- 1963 *Stigma* Englewood Cliffs, NJ: Prentice-Hall

Gold, Martin 1970 *Delinquent Behavior in an American City* Belmont, Cal: Brooks

Gordon, Robert A. 1980 'Research on IQ, Race and Delinquency: Taboo or Not Taboo?' in Edward Sagarin ed *Taboos in Criminology* Beverly Hills, Cal: Sage Publications, 37–66

Gottfredson, Don M., Leslie T. Wilkins and Peter B. Hoffman 1978 *Guidelines for Parole and Sentencing* Lexington, Mass: D.C. Heath

Gottfredson, Michael R. 1974 'An Empirical Analysis of Pre-trial Release Decisions' *Journal of Criminal Justice* 2(4):287–304

- 1979 'Parole Guidelines and the Reduction of Sentencing Disparity: A Preliminary Study' *Journal of Research in Crime and Delinquency* 16(2):218–45

Gottfredson, Stephen D. and Don M. Gottfredson 1979 'Screening for Risk: A Comparison of Methods' paper presented at the American Society of Criminology meetings, Philadelphia, November

Greenberg, David F. 1979 *Mathematical Criminology* New Brunswick, NJ: Rutgers University Press

Greenland, Cyril 1984 'Dangerous Sexual Offender Legislation in Canada, 1948–77: An Experiment that Failed' *Canadian Journal of Criminology*, 26(1):1–12

Greenwood, Peter W., with Abrahamse, Allan 1982 *Selective Incapacitation* Santa Monica, Cal: Rand Corporation

Greenwood, Peter W., Joan Petersilia and Franklin E. Zimring 1980 *Age, Crime and Sanctions: The Transition from Juvenile to Adult Court* Santa Monica, Cal: Rand Corporation

Gurr, Ted 1968 'Urban Disorder: Perspectives from the Comparative Study of Civil Strife' in Louis H. Masotti and Don R. Bowen eds *Riots and Rebellion: Civil Violence in the Urban Community* Beverly Hills, Cal: Sage Publications

Guze, Samuel B. 1976 *Criminality and Psychiatric Disorders* New York: Oxford University Press

Hafen, B.Q. ed 1968 *Drug Abuse: Psychology, Sociology, Pharmacology* Provo, Utah: Brigham Young University Press

Hagan, John L. 1974 'Extra-Legal Attributes and Criminal Sentencing: An Assessment of a Sociological Viewpoint' *Law and Society Review* 8:357–83

Halleck, Seymour 1967 *Psychiatry and the Dilemmas of Crime* New York: Harper and Row

Hamparian, Donna M., Richard Schuster, Simon Dinitz and John P. Conrad 1978 *The Violent Few: A Study of Dangerous Juvenile Offenders* Lexington, Mass: D.C. Heath

Handlin, Oscar 1962 *The Newcomers: Negroes and Puerto Ricans in a Changing Metropolis* Garden City, NY: Doubleday

Hare, Robert D. 1970 *Psychopathy: Theory and Research* New York: Wiley

Harris, Carl M. and Soumyo D. Moitra 1978 'Improved Statistical Techniques for the Measurement of Recidivism' *Journal of Research in Crime and Delinquency* 15:194–213

Hartnagel, Timothy 1978 'The Effect of Age and Sex Composition of Provincial Populations on Provincial Crime Rates' *Canadian Journal of Criminology* 20(1):28–33

Hasenpusch, Burkhard 1978 'The Rise and Fall of Crime in Canada: An Attempt at Criminological Forecasting' *Crime and Justice* 6(2):108–23

Hawkins, Gordon 1976 *The Prison: Policy and Practice* Chicago: University of Chicago Press

Heilburn, A.B., I.J. Knopf and P. Brunner 'Criminal Impulsivity and Violence and Subsequent Parole Outcome' *British Journal of Criminology* 16(4):367–77

Hindelang, Michael 1976 *Criminal Victimization in Eight American Cities* Cambridge, Mass: Ballinger

Hindelang, Michael, Travis Hirschi and Joseph Weis 1981 *Measuring Delinquency* Beverly Hills, Cal: Sage Publications

Hirschi, Travis 1969 *Causes of Delinquency* Berkeley, Cal: University of California Press

Hirschi, Travis and Michael Gottfredson 1983 'Age and the Explanation of Crime' *American Journal of Sociology* 89(3):552–84

Hogarth, John 1971 *Sentencing as a Human Process* Toronto: University of Toronto Press

Inciardi, James A. ed 1981 *The Drugs-Crime Connection* Beverly Hills, Cal: Sage

Irwin, John 1970 *The Felon* Englewood Cliffs, NJ: Prentice-Hall

Jacobs, James B. 1974 'Street Gangs behind Bars' *Social Problems* 21:395–409

Jacobs, Jane 1961 *The Death and Life of Great American Cities* New York: Vintage

Jaffary, Stuart 1963 *The Sentencing of Adults in Canada* Toronto: University of Toronto Press

Jaman, Dorothy, R., Robert R. Dickover and Lawrence A. Bennett 1972 'Parole Outcome as a Function of Time Served' *British Journal of Criminology* 12(1):5–31

Jeffery, Clarence R. 1977 *Crime Prevention through Environmental Design* Beverly Hills, Cal: Sage

– 1979 *Biology and Crime* Beverly Hills, Cal: Sage

Jones, Bryan D. 1980 'The Advocate, the Auditor and the Program Manager: Statistical Decision Theory and Human Service Programs' *Evaluation Review* 4:275–305

Jones, Ernest T. 1973 'Evaluating Everyday Policies: Police Activity and Crime Incidence' *Urban Affairs Quarterly* 8:267–79

- 1974 'The Impact of Crime Rate Changes on Police Protection Expenditures in American Cities' *Criminology* 11:516-24

Juvenile Court Judges of Ohio 1979 *Placement Model Information* Sydney, Ohio: Juvenile Judge's Conference

Kalman, Gyorgyi 1981 'The New Penal Code' *Hungarian Digest* March, 98-103

Khleif, B.B. 1964 'Teachers as Predictors of Juvenile Delinquency and Psychiatric Disturbance' *Social Problems* 11:270-82

Klecka, William R. 1975 'Discriminant Analysis' in Norman Nie, C. Hadlai Hull, Jean Jenkins, Karin Steinbrenner, and Dale Brent eds *Statistical Package for the Social Sciences* New York: McGraw-Hill

Kolb, Lawrence C. 1973 *Modern Clinical Psychiatry* 8th edition Philadelphia, Pa: W.B. Saunders

Kornblum, Charlene S. 1979 *Fourth Year Evaluation of the City of Seattle's Community Crime Prevention Program* Seattle: Law and Justice Planning Office

Kozol, Harry, Richard Boucher and Ralph Garofalo 1972 'The Diagnosis and Treatment of Dangerousness' *Crime and Delinquency* 18(4):371-92

Kratcoski, P. 1974 'Differential Treatment of Delinquent Boys and Girls in Juvenile Court' *Child Welfare* 53:16-22

Kurtzberg, Richard L., Michael Lewin, Norman Cavior and Douglas Lipton 1967 'Psychological Screening of Inmates Requesting Cosmetic Operations: A Preliminary Report' *Plastic and Reconstructive Surgery* 39(4):387-96

Land, Kenneth C. 1969 'Principles of Path Analysis' in Edgar F. Borgatta ed *Sociological Methodology 1969* San Francisco: Jossey-Bass

Lazarus, Richard and Edward Opton eds 1967 *Personality* London: Cox and Wyman

Leger, Robert and John Stratton eds 1977 *The Sociology of Corrections* New York: John Wiley and Sons

Lemert, Edwin M. 1967 *Human Deviance, Social Problems, and Social Control* Englewood Cliffs, NJ: Prentice-Hall

Lewis, Viola G., John Money, and Nanci A. Bobrow 1973 'Psychologic Study of Boys with Short Stature, Retarded Osseous Growth and Normal Age of Pubertal Onset' *Adolescence* 8(32):445-54

Lewis-Beck, Michael S. 1980 *Applied Regression: An Introduction* Beverly Hills, Cal: Sage

Lieberson, Stanley and Arnold R. Silverman 1965 'The Precipitants and Underlying Conditions of Race Riots' *American Sociological Review* 30:887-98

Loeber, R. and T. Dishion 1983 'Early Predictors of Male Delinquency: A Review' *Psychological Bulletin* 94(1):68-99

Luedtke, George and Associates 1970 *Crime and the Physical City:*

Neighborhood Design Techniques for Crime Reduction Washington, DC:
National Institute of Law Enforcement and Criminal Justice

McBride, Duane C. 1981 'Drugs and Violence' in James A. Inciardi ed *The
Drugs-Crime Connection* Beverly Hills, Cal: Sage, 105–23

McCord, William and Joan McCord 1964 *The Psychopath: An Essay on the
Criminal Mind* New York: Van Nostrand Reinhold

McKay, H. Bryan, C.H.S. Jayewardene, and Penny B. Reedie 1979 *The Effects
of Long-Term Incarceration* Ottawa: The Solicitor General of Canada

Mannheim, Hermann 1965 *Comparative Criminology* Boston: Houghton Mifflin

Mannheim, Hermann and Leslie T. Wilkins 1955 *Prediction Methods in Relation
to Borstal Training* London: Her Majesty's Stationery Office

Martin, John M. and Joseph P. Fitzpatrick 1964 *Delinquent Behavior: A
Redefinition of the Problem* New York: Random House

Martinson, Robert 1972 'Collective Behavior at Attica' *Federal Probation*
36(3):3–7

Marx, Karl and Friedrich Engels 1955 'Wage Labour and Capital' in *Selected
Works in Two Volumes* Moscow: Foreign Languages Publishing House, vol. 1

Masotti, Louis H. and Don R. Bowen 1968 *Riots and Rebellion: Civil Violence in
the Urban Community* Beverly Hills, Cal: Sage

Masters, F.W. and D.C. Greaves 1967 'The Quasimodo Complex' *British Journal
of Plastic Surgery* 20:204–10

Matza, David 1966 *Delinquency and Drift* New York: Wiley

Meade, A. 1973 'Seriousness of Delinquency, the Adjudicative Decision and
Recidivism: A Longitudinal Configuration Analysis' *Journal of Criminal Law
and Criminology* 64:478–85

Mednick, Sarnoff A. and Jan Volavka 1980 'Biology and Crime' in Norval
Morris and Michael Tonry eds *Crime and Justice: An Annual Review of
Research* Chicago: University of Chicago Press, 85–158

Meehl, Paul 1954 *Clinical versus Statistical Prediction: A Theoretical Analysis
and a Review of the Evidence* Minneapolis, Minn: University of Minnesota
Press

Meehl, Paul and A. Rosen 1955 'Antecedent Probability and the Efficacy of
Psychometric Signs, Patterns or Cutting Scores' *Psychological Bulletin*
52:194–216

Megargee, Edwin I. and Martin J. Bohn 1979 *Classifying Criminal Offenders: A
New System Based on the MMPI* Beverly Hills, Cal: Sage

Menzies, Robert J., Christopher P. Webster and Diana S. Sepejak 1982 *'At the
Mercy of the Mad': Examining the Relationship between Violence and Mental
Illness* Toronto: Metfors

Merker, Phillip C. 1968 'General Aspects of Pharmacology' in B.Q. Hafen ed

Drug Abuse: Psychology, Sociology, Pharmacology Provo, Utah: Brigham Young University Press

Merton, Robert K. 1968 *Social Theory and Social Structure* New York: MacMillan

Miller, Walter B. 1958 'Lower Class Structure as a Generating Milieu of Gang Delinquency' *Journal of Social Issues* 14(3):5–19

Mitford, Jessica 1974 *Kind and Unusual Punishment: The Prison Business* New York: Random House

Monahan, John 1975 'The Prediction of Violence' in Duncan Chappel ed *Violence and Criminal Justice* Lexington, Mass: D.C. Heath, 15–32

– 1981 *Predicting Violent Behavior: An Assessment of Clinical Techniques* Beverly Hills, Cal: Sage

– 1982 'The Case for Prediction in the Modified Desert Model of Criminal Sentencing' *International Journal of Law and Psychiatry* 5:103–13

– 1984 'The Prediction of Violent Behavior: Toward a Second Generation of Theory and Policy' *American Journal of Psychiatry* 141(1):10–15

Monahan, John and Henry J. Steadman 1983 'Crime and Mental Disorder: An Epidemiological Approach' in Michael Tonry and Norval Morris eds *Crime and Justice: An Annual Review of Research, Volume 4* Chicago: University of Chicago Press, 145–89

Moos, Rudolph H. 1975 *Evaluating Correctional and Community Settings* New York: John Wiley

Morrison, Denton, E. 1971 'Some Notes toward a Theory on Relative Deprivation, Social Movements and Social Change' *American Behavioral Scientist* 15(5):675–90

Moses, Earl R. 1947 'Differentials in Crime Rates between Negroes and Whites Based on Comparisons of Four Socioeconomically Equated Areas' *American Sociological Review* 12(4):411–20

Moyer, Kenneth 1979 'What Is the Potential for Biological Violence Control?' in Clarence R. Jeffery ed *Biology and Crime* Beverly Hills, Cal: Sage, 19–46

Nagel, Ilene H. and John Hagan 1983 'Gender and Crime: Offense Patterns and Criminal Court Sanctions' in Michael Tonry and Norval Morris eds *Crime and Justice: An Annual Review of Research, Volume 4* Chicago: University of Chicago Press, 91–144

Nagel, Stuart S. and Marian G. Neef 1979 *Decision Theory and the Legal Process* Lexington, Mass: D.C. Heath

National Crime Panel 1974 *Criminal Victimization in the United States, January–June, 1973* Washington, DC: U.S. Department of Justice

Neithercutt, M.G. 1972 'Parole Violation Patterns and Commitment Offence' *Journal of Research in Crime and Delinquency* 9:87–98

Neter, John and William Wasserman 1974 *Applied Linear Statistical Models* Homewood, Ill: Richard D. Irwin

Nettler, Gwynn 1978 *Explaining Crime* New York: McGraw-Hill

Newman, Oscar 1972 *Defensible Space* New York: Macmillan

Newsweek 1981 'Can a Family Corrupt?' 11 May p 75

Nie, Norman, C. Hadlai Hull, Jean Jenkins, Karin Steinbrenner and Dale Bent eds 1975 *Statistical Package for the Social Sciences* New York: McGraw-Hill

Nuffield, Joan 1982 *Parole Decision-Making in Canada: Research towards Decision Guidelines* Ottawa: Ministry of the Solicitor General

Ohlin, Lloyd E. 1951 *Selection for Parole* New York: Russel Sage Foundation

Ozanne, Marq R., Robert A. Wilson and Dewaine L. Gedney 1980 'Toward a Theory of Bail Risk' *Criminology* 18(2):147-61

Packer, Herbert L. 1968 *The Limits of the Criminal Sanction* Stanford, Cal: Stanford University Press

Palmer, Jan and Paul Carlson 1978 'Problems with the Use of Regression Analysis in Prediction Studies' *Journal of Research in Crime and Delinquency* 15(1):92-198

Petersilia, Joan, Peter W. Greenwood, and Martin Lavin 1977 *Criminal Careers of Habitual Felons* Santa Monica, Cal: Rand Corporation

Peterson, Mark, Harriet Braiker and S. Polich 1980 *Doing Crime: A Survey of California Prison Inmates* Santa Monica, Cal: Rand Corporation

Petrunik, Michael 1980 *Legal Controls for Dangerous Persons in Europe and North America* Ottawa: Ministry of the Solicitor General of Canada

Pfohl, Stephen 1977 'The Psychiatric Assessment of Dangerousness: Practical Problems and Political Implications' in Simon Dinitz and John Conrad eds *In Fear of Each Other* Lexington, Mass: D.C. Heath

Piliavin, Irving and Scott Briar 1964 'Police Encounters with Juveniles' *American Journal of Sociology* 70:206-14

Powers, Edwin and Helen Witmer 1951 *An Experiment in the Prevention of Delinquency* New York: Columbia University Press

Quarantelli, E.L. and Russell R. Dynes 1975 'Organizations as Victims in American Mass Racial Disturbances: A Re-examination' in Israel Drapkin and Emilio Viano eds *Victimology: A New Focus* Lexington, Mass: D.C. Heath

Quetelet, Adolphe 1833 *Recherches sur le penchant au crime aux différents ages* Brussels

Quinsey, Vernon L. 1980 'The Baserate Problem and the Prediction of Dangerousness: A Reappraisal' *The Journal of Psychiatry and Law* 8:329-40

Quinsey, Vernon L. and Rudolf Ambtman 1979 'Variables Affecting Psychiatrists' and Teachers' Assessments of the Dangerousness of Mentally Ill Offenders' *Journal of Consulting and Clinical Psychology* 47(2):353-62

Radzinowicz, Leon and Joan King 1977 *The Growth of Crime: The International Experience* London: Cox and Wyman

Reckless, Walter C. 1961 *The Crime Problem* New York: Appleton-Century-Crofts

Reckless, Walter C. and Simon Dinitz 1972 *The Prevention of Juvenile Delinquency: An Experiment* Columbus, Ohio: Ohio State University Press

Reppetto, Thomas A. 1974 *Residential Crime* Cambridge, Mass: Ballinger

– 1976 'Crime Prevention and the Displacement Phenomenon' *Crime and Delinquency* 22:166–77

Robinson, W.S. 1950 'Ecological Correlations and the Behavior of Individuals' *American Sociological Review* 15:351–6

Roth, L. and R. Ervin 1971 'Psychiatric Care of Federal Prisoners' *American Journal of Psychiatry* 1128:424–30

Rubington, Earl 1969 'Types of Alcoholic Offenders' *Federal Probation* 33(1):28–35

Rummel, R.J. 1970 *Applied Factor Analysis* Evanston, Ill: Northwestern University Press

Rutter, Michael and Henri Giller 1983 *Juvenile Delinquency: Trends and Perspectives* New York: Penguin Books

Sagarin, Edward 1980 *Taboos in Criminology* Beverly Hills, Cal: Sage

Sagi, Phillip C. and Charles F. Wellford 1968 'Age Composition and Patterns of Change in Criminal Statistics' *Journal of Criminal Law, Criminology and Police Science* 59(1):29–36

Sampson, Allan 1974 'Post-prison Success Prediction: A Preliminary Florida Study' *Criminology* 12(2):155–73

Sawyer, J. 1966 'Measurement and Prediction: Clinical and Statistical' *Psychological Bulletin* 66:178–200

Schmid, Calvin F. 1960 'Urban Crime Areas' *American Sociological Review* 15:527–42, 655–78

Schuessler, Karl and Donald Cressey 1950 'Personality Characteristics of Criminals' *American Journal of Sociology* 55:476–84

Scott, Joseph E. 1974 'The Use of Discretion in Determining the Severity of Punishment for Incarcerated Offenders' *Journal of Criminal Law and Criminology* 65(2):214–24

Sellin, Thorsten and Marvin E. Wolfgang 1964 *The Measurement of Delinquency* New York: John Wiley

Shannon, Lyle 1980 *Assessing the Relationship of Adult Criminal Careers to Juvenile Careers* Iowa City, Iowa: Iowa Urban Community Research Center, University of Iowa

Shattuck, John H.F. and David E. Landau 1981 'Civil Liberties and Criminal

Code Reform' *The Journal of Criminal Law and Criminology* 72:914–54

Shaw, Clifford and Henry McKay 1942 *Juvenile Delinquency and Urban Areas* Chicago: University of Chicago Press

Shoham, S. 1966 'The Procedures and Sentencing Powers of the Criminal Courts in Israel' *Crime and Social Deviation* Chicago: Henry Regnery, 166–89

Sigall, Harold and Nancy Ostrove 1975 'Beautiful but Dangerous: Effects of Offender Attractiveness and Nature of the Crime on Juridic Judgement' *Journal of Personality and Social Psychology* 31(3):410–14

Silberman, Charles E. 1978 *Criminal Violence, Criminal Justice* New York: Vintage

Simon, Frances H. 1971 *Prediction Methods in Criminology* London: Her Majesty's Stationery Office

Simon, Rita J. 1975 *Women and Crime* Lexington, Mass: D.C. Heath

Singer, Richard 1979 *Just Deserts: Sentencing Based on Equality and Desert* Cambridge, Mass: Ballinger

Singh, Avtar, Halena Celinski and C.H.S. Jayewardene 1980 'Ecological Correlates of Crime in Ottawa' *Canadian Journal of Criminology* 22(1):78–85

Smart, Carol 1976 *Women, Crime and Criminology* London: Routledge and Kegan Paul

Solomon, Herbert 1976 'Parole Outcome: A Multidimensional Contingency Table Analysis' *Journal of Research in Crime and Delinquency* 13:107–26

Steadman, H. and C. Keveles 'The Community Adjustment and Criminal Activity of the Baxstrom Patients: 1966–70' *American Journal of Psychiatry* 129:304–10

Sykes, Gresham M. 1956 *Crime and Society* New York: Random House

Teilmann, Katherine A. and Pierre H. Landry 1981 'Gender Bias in Juvenile Justice' *Journal of Research in Crime and Delinquency* 18(1):47–80

Toch, Hans 1980 *Violent Men* Cambridge, Mass: Schenkman

Transport Canada, Standards Evaluation and Statistical Analysis Section 1981 *State of the Art Review, Risk Analysis* Ottawa: Transport Canada

Tyrpak, Steven 1975 *Newark High Impact Anti-Crime Program: Street Lighting Project Interim Evaluation Report* Newark, NJ: Office of Criminal Justice Planning

Van Alstyne, David J. and Michael R. Gottfredson 1978 'A Multi-dimensional Contingency Table Analysis of Parole Outcome: New Methods and Old Problems in Criminological Prediction' *Journal of Research in Crime and Delinquency* 15(2):172–93

Vold, George 1958 *Theoretical Criminology* New York: Oxford University Press

– 1979 *Theoretical Criminology* 2nd edition, New York: Oxford University Press

Von Hirsch, Andrew 1976 *Doing Justice: The Choice of Punishment* New York: Hill and Wang

Waldo, Gordon P. and Simon Dinitz 1967 'Personality Attributes of the
  Criminal: An Analysis of Research Studies' *The Journal of Research in Crime
  and Delinquency* 4(2):185–202
Walker, Nigel 1965 *Crime and Punishment in Britain* Edinburgh: University of
  Edinburgh Press
– 1980 *Punishment, Danger and Stigma: The Morality of Criminal Justice*
  Totowa, NJ: Barnes and Noble
Waller, Irvin 1974 *Men Released from Prison* Toronto: University of Toronto
  Press
Waller, Irvin and Norm Okihiro 1978 *Burglary: The Victim and the Public*
  Toronto: University of Toronto Press
Weis, Kurt 1974 'The Glueck Social Prediction Table – An Unfulfilled Promise'
  The Journal of Criminal Law and Criminology 65:397–404
Wenk, Ernst, James Robinson and Gerald Smith 1972 'Can Violence Be
  Predicted?' *Crime and Delinquency* 18(4):393–402
Werner, Paul D., Terrence L. Rose and Jerome A. Yesavage 1983 'Reliability,
  Accuracy, and Decision-Making Strategy in Clinical Predictions of Imminent
  Dangerousness' *Journal of Consulting and Clinical Psychology* 51(6):815–25
West, D.J. 1967 *The Young Offender* London: Cox and Wyman
Wheeler, Stanton 1961 'Socialization in Correctional Communities' *American
  Sociological Review* 26:697–712
White, Clyde R. 1932 'The Relation of Felonies to Environmental Factors in
  Indianapolis' *Social Forces* 10(4):498–509
Wiggins, J.S. 1973 *Personality and Prediction: Principles of Personality
  Assessment* Don Mills, Ont: Addison-Wesley
Wilds, Charles, E. 1973 'Evaluation of a Method of Predicting Violence in
  Offenders' *Criminology* 11(3):427–35
Wilkins, Leslie T. 1960 *Delinquent Generation* London: Home Office Studies in
  the Causes of Delinquency and the Treatment of Offenders, No. 3
Wilkins, Leslie T. and Peter MacNaughton-Smith 1964 'New Prediction and
  Classification Methods in Criminology' *Journal of Research in Crime and
  Delinquency* 1:19–32
Williams, W.T. and J.M. Lambert 1959 'Multivariate Methods in Plant Ecology'
  Journal of Ecology 47:83–101
Wilson, James Q. 1975 *Thinking about Crime* New York: Basic Books
Wilson, James Q. and Richard J. Herrnstein 1985 *Crime and Human Nature* New
  York: Simon and Schuster
Wolfgang, Marvin E. 1958 *Patterns in Criminal Homicide* Philadelphia:
  University of Pennsylvania
– 1977 'From Boy to Man – From Delinquency to Crime' paper presented to the

National Symposium on the Serious Juvenile Offender, Minneapolis, Minn: Department of Corrections

- 1985 'The Longitudinal Study of Delinquency and Crime' paper presented at the Fourth Asian-Pacific Conference on Juvenile Delinquency, Tokyo-Kobe, Japan, 11 November

Wolfgang, Marvin E. and Franco Ferracuti 1967 *The Subculture of Violence* London: Tavistock

Wolfgang, Marvin E. and Franco Ferracuti 1967 *The Subculture of Violence* London: Tavistock

Wolfgang, Marvin E., Robert M. Figlio and Thorsten Sellin 1972 *Delinquency in a Birth Cohort* Chicago: University of Chicago Press

Yochelson, Samuel and Stanton E. Samenow 1976 *The Criminal Personality* New York: Jason Aronsen

Zajac, A.S. 1968 'Biological and Psychodynamic Positions and Treatment' *Canadian Journal of Corrections* 10(1):25-40

Zawadzki, B. and Paul F. Lazarsfeld 1935 'The Psychological Consequences of Unemployment' *Journal of Social Psychology* 6:224-51

Zimring, Franklin E. 1981 'Kids, Groups and Crime: Some Implications of a Well-Known Secret' *Journal of Criminal Law and Criminology* 72(3):867-85

Zingraff, Matthew T. 1975 'Prisonization as an Inhibitor of Effective Resocialization' *Criminology* 13(30):366-81

Zitrin, A., A. Hardesty, E. Burdock and J. Drosaman 1976 'Crime and Violence among Mental Patients' *American Journal of Psychiatry* 133:142-9

Author index

Subject index

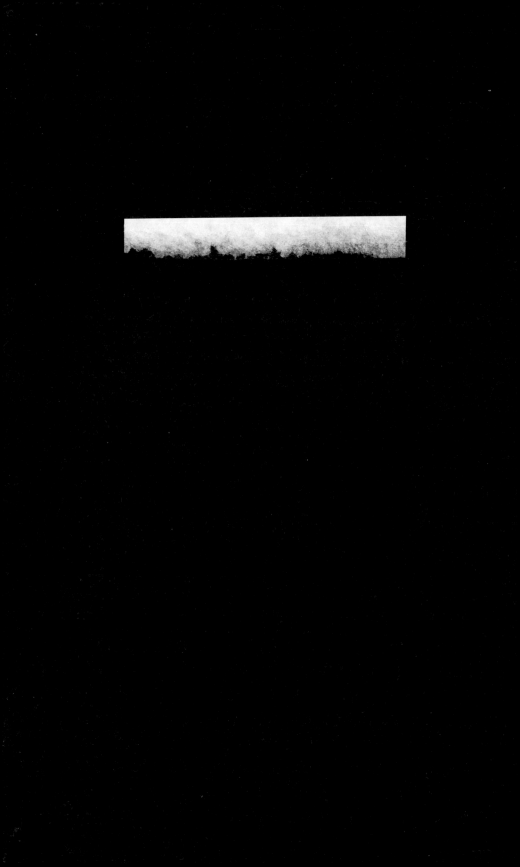